Cooking School

ITALIAN

Cooking School

ITALIAN

Bring the flavors of Italy to life in your own kitchen!

This edition published in 2010
LOVE FOOD is an imprint of Parragon Books Ltd

Parragon
Queen Street House
4 Queen Street
Bath BA1 1HE, UK

ISBN: 978-1-4075-9479-8

Printed in China

Internal design by Pink Creative
Additional internal photography by Charlie Richards*
Internal food styling by Mary Wall
Internal prop styling by Sarah Waller
Introduction by Christine McFadden

Notes for the Reader

This book uses imperial, metric, and US cup measurements. Follow the same units of measurement throughout; do not mix imperial and metric. All spoon measurements are level: teaspoons are assumed to be 5 ml, and tablespoons are assumed to be 15 ml. Unless otherwise stated, milk is assumed to be whole, eggs and individual vegetables, such as potatoes, are medium, and pepper is freshly ground black pepper.

The times given are an approximate guide only. Preparation times differ according to the techniques used by different people and the cooking times may also vary from those given as a result of the type of oven used. Optional ingredients, variations, or serving suggestions have not been included in the calculations.

Recipes using raw or very lightly cooked eggs should be avoided by infants, the elderly, pregnant women, convalescents, and anyone with a chronic condition. Pregnant and breastfeeding women are advised to avoid eating peanuts and peanut products. People with nut allergies should be aware that some of the prepared ingredients used in the recipes in this book may contain nuts. Always check the packaging before use.

* pages 6, 7, 12, 46, 50, 66, 74, 77, 81, 82, 86, 94, 98, 102, 120, 127, 154, 166, 185 & 186

Contents

Introduction

As a nation with one of the longest and most complex culinary histories, the Italians take their cuisine seriously. It is an innate part of the culture and plays an important role in local traditions and history. Cooking and eating are synonymous with conviviality, good company, and good wine, and for most Italians life revolves around mealtimes, whether eaten at home or at one of the many types of restaurant.

Despite increasingly busy lifestyles, many Italians still make daily trips to the local market or delicatessen to buy the freshest and best produce available. Although ingredients are available year-round, Italians have always preferred to eat locally grown foods at the time of year when they are fully ripe and the flavor is at its best—a concept other developed countries are only just beginning to adopt.

Regional Variations

Before Italy's unification in 1870, the country was made up of numerous small republics and kingdoms, each area being a tightly knit community with its own particular cuisine. What was eaten depended on geographical region as well as culture.

In the fertile plains of the north, dairy products and beef were common. Even today, butter is used more than oil for cooking and many sauces are based on cream or cheese made from cow's milk. In the hot and arid south, the diet was more frugal, based on olive oil, vegetables, fish, and cheeses made from sheep or goat milk. Coastal areas obviously made best use of seafood, while in mountainous areas cured meats that could be stored for long periods were an important part of the cuisine.

Rice was an important staple in Lombardy, the Po Valley, and the Venetian hinterland. Along with polenta, it was considered the food of the poor and was often combined with simple ingredients, such as in Risotto Primavera. Baked polenta was another plain but sustaining dish that made the most of whatever ingredients were on hand. Nowadays, both rice and polenta continue to feature prominently on regional menus in restaurants, ranging from the most basic *osteria* to the grandest *trattoria*.

Each region had, and still has, its own bread: big-holed, chewy ciabatta in the north; dense, unsalted white bread in Tuscany; and gigantic, crusty wheels of rough country bread in Puglia in the south.

Likewise, pasta has regional variations. In the north, it is often freshly made with egg—perfect for absorbing creamy sauces. In the south, the pasta is hard and dry, made only with durum wheat and water. This type is more suitable for oil- or tomato-based sauces.

Although similar dishes are now found throughout the country, thanks to modern food-storage and transport systems, each of Italy's 20 regions remains fiercely proud of its individual culinary identity. True to form, Italians continue to be strongly attached to authentic food and long-held culinary traditions, while at the same time making the most of contemporary tastes and new ideas.

Essential Italian Ingredients

Most basic Italian ingredients can be stored for months. As you build up your supplies, you'll always have the makings of a delicious meal.

OLIVE OIL

Graded according to international standards, the lower the acidity the better the flavor. It should be stored in a cool, dark place and is best bought in cans or dark bottles.

Extra virgin, first cold-pressed: The finest grade, with a superb, peppery flavor and fruity aroma. Use it for dressing salads and broiled vegetables, and for dipping bread.

Virgin: The next-best grade after extra virgin, with a reasonable flavor. Use it for cooking rather than in dressings.

Olive oil, or pure olive oil: A blend of refined, virgin, and extra virgin oils, with a bland flavor.

CHEESES

Fontina: Smooth cow's milk cheese for melting into sauces and gratins. It has a sweet, buttery, mild flavor.

Gorgonzola: A sharp, creamy blue cheese made from cow's milk with excellent flavoring for pasta sauces and soups, and also served as a table cheese.

Mascarpone: Cow's milk cream cheese with a high fat content (40–50 percent), used for enriching pasta sauces, baked dishes, and desserts.

Mozzarella: Slightly stringy, milky white cheese that melts well—the best is made from water buffalo's milk, but cow's milk mozzarella is more widely available. Use it fresh in salads, as a pizza topping, or baked in lasagna.

Parmigiano-Reggiano (Parmesan): A hard, cow's milk cheese made to a strict traditional formula, it has a complex nutty flavor and a slightly crystalline texture. It is used mainly for grating, although it is also served as a table cheese when moist and young. Always grate just before using.

Pecorino Romano (pecorino): A hard, sheep milk cheese with a crumbly texture and sharp flavor, used as a grating cheese.

Ricotta: A soft, fresh, unsalted cheese made with cow's milk whey, it has a mild flavor suitable for both savory and sweet dishes. Use it for stuffed pasta, dips, sauces, pastries, and tarts.

MEATS—CURED

Pancetta: An Italian bacon sold cubed or in thin slices.

Parma ham: A pale, sweet-tasting ham, it must come from pigs weighing more than 330 lb/150 kg and must be air-dried in specific regions of northern Italy.

Salami: This comes in an enormous variety of sizes and flavorings with regional specialties.

FISH AND SEAFOOD—CURED

Anchovies: Brine-cured or salted fillets, used in pizza, salads, dips, and sauces, and for flavoring meat and vegetable dishes. Anchovies deepen other flavors without imparting a fishy taste.

Clams: Available in cans or jars. Add to pasta sauces or risotto.

Tuna: Packed in oil or brine, invaluable for salads and pasta sauces.

PASTA—DRIED

There are two basic types: pasta made with hard durum wheat flour (semolina) and water, and egg pasta made with all-purpose flour and eggs. Pasta comes in an extraordinary number of shapes, each lending itself to a particular type of sauce. Long, round pasta is best with tomato- or oil-based sauces that cling to the pasta; tubes and shapes are ideal for trapping chunkier sauces in their crevices. Egg pasta is more absorbent and best with butter- or cream-based sauces.

RISOTTO RICE

The short oval grains of risotto rice have a high starch content, which gives risotto its characteristic creaminess. Arborio is the best-known variety, but vialone nano and carnaroli are also both widely used.

POLENTA

A staple food in Northern Italy, polenta is made from coarsely ground cornmeal. Depending on the amount of water added, polenta is served wet, like mashed potatoes, or cooled and cut into shapes for broiling, baking, or frying.

LEGUMES

Beans, lentils, and chickpeas are used throughout Italy but are particularly popular in Tuscany and Umbria. They are sold dried or in cans; dried legumes need lengthy soaking and cooking but have a better flavor.

HERBS

Fresh herbs are best but, if necessary, rosemary, thyme, sage, marjoram, and oregano may be used dried. Make sure you buy chopped dried leaves instead of ground, powdered herbs. Use 1 teaspoon of dried herbs in place of 1 tablespoon of fresh herbs.

PINE NUTS

Oily, cream-colored kernels with a slightly sweet flavor, pine nuts are an essential ingredient in pesto, and are also used in cookies and cakes.

Hints and Tips

Italian cooking is wonderfully straightforward but it is worth mastering a few tricks of the trade to increase your confidence.

Making Fresh Pasta Dough

- Unlike pastry, pasta responds well to warmth. Never work on a marble board; instead use a large wooden board or other smooth, relatively warm material.
- For the best results use Italian "00" flour, but if you can't find it, you can use all-purpose flour.
- Rolling by hand: Knead the dough for at least 10–15 minutes, until smooth and elastic. Roll out on a floured cloth as thinly and evenly as possible until the weave of the cloth shows through.
- Rolling by machine: Feed strips of dough repeatedly through the rollers, closing them one notch at a time to gradually thin the dough. This is time-consuming but necessary—resist the urge to skip a notch.

Cooking Pasta

- Use a pan that is large enough to allow the pasta to move around and swell.
- There is no need to add oil to the cooking water if you use enough water. Use 4 cups water and 1 teaspoon salt for every 3½ oz/100 g pasta.
- Never cook more than 2 lb 4 oz/1 kg pasta in the same pan.

Making Polenta

- Dry cornmeal is poured into boiling salted water and stirred vigorously until the desired consistency is reached. Cooking times vary, so always check the package directions.
- Consistency depends on the ratio of water to cornmeal:

  Stiff: 2 parts water/1 part cornmeal.

  Medium: 5 parts water/1 part cornmeal.

  Soft: 7 parts water/1 part cornmeal.
- Stir in the cornmeal a handful at a time. To prevent lumps, make sure each handful is absorbed before adding the next. The polenta is ready when it comes away from the sides of the pan.
- To serve wet: Spoon into a serving dish.
- To serve dry: Spread out in a shallow roasting pan and level with a wet palette knife. Let stand until firm then slice into the desired shape.
- To broil: Place polenta slices in a broiler pan and brush both sides with olive oil. Broil for 5–7 minutes, until golden and crisp at the edges. Turn and broil the other side.

Making Risotto

- Use a wide, heavy-bottom pan.
- Do not wash risotto rice—the starch from the grains is an essential part of the dish.
- Make sure the stock is hot before you add it to the rice. It's best to keep it simmering in a small pan.
- Add a ladleful of cooking liquid at a time, and stir until the liquid disappears before adding the next.

Making Bread and Pizza Dough

- Always sift the flour first to remove any lumps and to incorporate air into the flour. Add the specified amount of salt to the flour when sifting to distribute it evenly.
- Yeast thrives in warm surroundings. Make sure all the ingredients and equipment are warm before you begin.
- To make lukewarm water, use 1 part boiling to 2 parts cold.
- The amount of liquid needed may vary from the quantity stated in the recipe; it depends on the type of flour and the amount of moisture in the air. You need enough liquid to make the dough soft but not too sticky. Always hold back a little of the flour and water so you can adjust the consistency as necessary.
- Knead the dough for at least 10 minutes, until it feels silky smooth and elastic.
- After kneading, let the dough rise in a lightly oiled, deep bowl. Oiling lets the dough rise smoothly without sticking to the sides of the bowl.
- Bake pizza at the highest possible temperature in the top of a preheated oven. Using a preheated pizza stone produces the crispest results. Otherwise use a perforated pizza pan—the holes let heat and air reach the bottom of the dough.

Antipasti and Soups

Antipasti have been part of Italian culture for centuries. Literally meaning "before the meal" (from *pasto*, meaning "meal"), the term refers to hot or cold appetizers served before the first course. Antipasti usually come in three categories—vegetables, meat, and fish—and range from a simply prepared vegetable or salad to more elaborate meat and seafood dishes. Vegetables may be served raw for dipping in a garlicky Bagna Calda, or marinated in oil or pickled to accompany cured meats. There are seemingly endless varieties of cured meats with a rich variety of textures and flavors. Some of the best antipasti are made with fish and seafood. Crisp and succulent Pan-Fried Shrimp are one of the favorites, while economical fish, such as fresh and dried anchovies and sardines, appear in many guises.

Soups play an important part in Italian cuisine. They vary in consistency from light and delicate broths to hearty, meal-in-a-bowl soups that you almost need a knife and fork to eat. Soups are generally served warm in Italy instead of piping hot. Texture is always apparent—Italians rarely serve smooth soups. Some may be partially pureed but the identity of the ingredients is never entirely obliterated. There are regional characteristics, too. In the north, soups are often based on rice, while tomato, garlic, and pasta soups are typical of the south. Popular in Tuscany are thick bean- or bread-based soups, such as Bread and Tomato Soup and Ribollita, a hearty mixture of vegetables and beans with pieces of bread stirred in. They are the perfect way to use up bread that has become slightly stale.

Bruschetta with Tomatoes

SERVES 4

10½ oz/300 g cherry tomatoes

4 sun-dried tomatoes

4 tbsp extra virgin olive oil

16 fresh basil leaves, shredded, plus extra
   leaves to garnish

8 slices ciabatta

2 garlic cloves, cut in half lengthwise

salt and pepper

1. Using a sharp knife, cut the cherry tomatoes in half and the sun-dried tomatoes into strips. Place
    them in a bowl, add the oil and the shredded basil leaves, and toss to mix well. Season to taste with
    salt and pepper.

2. Preheat the broiler to medium, then lightly toast both sides of the ciabatta.

3. Rub the garlic, cut-side down, over both sides of the toasted ciabatta.

4. Top the ciabatta with the tomato mixture, garnish with basil leaves, and serve immediately.

Crostini alla Fiorentina

SERVES 6

3 tbsp olive oil

1 onion, chopped

1 celery stalk, chopped

1 carrot, chopped

1–2 garlic cloves, crushed

4½ oz/125 g chicken livers

4½ oz/125 g calf, lamb, or pork liver

⅔ cup red wine

1 tbsp tomato paste

2 tbsp chopped fresh flat-leaf parsley, plus extra sprigs to garnish

3–4 canned anchovy fillets, drained and finely chopped

2 tbsp stock or water

2–3 tbsp butter

1 tbsp capers, plus extra to garnish

12 slices ciabatta

salt and pepper

1. Heat the oil in a pan, add the onion, celery, carrot, and garlic and cook gently for 4–5 minutes, or until the onion is softened but not colored.

2. Meanwhile, rinse and dry the chicken livers. Rinse and dry the calf liver and slice into strips. Add both types of liver to the pan and fry gently for a few minutes, until sealed on all sides.

3. Add half of the wine and cook until it has almost evaporated. Add the remaining wine, the tomato paste, half the parsley, the anchovy fillets, stock, a little salt, and plenty of pepper.

4. Cover the pan and let simmer, stirring occasionally, for 15–20 minutes, or until the liver is tender and most of the liquid has been absorbed.

5. Let the mixture cool a little, then put into a food processor and process to a chunky paste.

6. Return to the pan and add the butter, capers, and the remaining parsley. Heat through gently until the butter melts. Adjust the seasoning, adding salt and pepper if needed, and turn out into a bowl. Cover and let cool before serving, if desired.

7. Preheat the broiler to medium, then lightly toast both sides of the ciabatta. Spread the liver mixture, warm or cold, over the toasted ciabatta, garnish with parsley sprigs and capers, and serve.

Deep-Fried Mozzarella Sandwiches

SERVES 4

8 slices white bread, preferably 1–2 days old,
  crusts removed

3½ oz/100 g mozzarella, thickly sliced

½ cup chopped black olives

8 canned anchovy fillets, drained and chopped

16 fresh basil leaves, plus extra sprigs
  to garnish

4 eggs, beaten

⅔ cup milk

oil, for deep-frying

salt and pepper

1. Cut each slice of bread into 2 triangles. Top 8 of the bread triangles with equal amounts of the mozzarella slices, olives, and anchovies. Place 2 of the basil leaves on top of each and season to taste with salt and pepper. Lay the other 8 triangles of bread over the top and press firmly around the edges to seal.

2. Mix the eggs and milk together and pour into a wide, shallow baking dish. Add the sandwiches and let soak for about 5 minutes.

3. Heat enough oil for deep-frying in a large saucepan to 350–375°F/180–190°C, or until a cube of bread browns in 30 seconds. Before cooking the sandwiches, squeeze the edges together again.

4. Carefully place the sandwiches in the oil and deep-fry, turning once, for 2 minutes, or until golden. (You will have to cook them in batches.) Remove with a slotted spoon and drain on paper towels. Serve immediately, garnished with basil sprigs.

Eggplant Rolls

SERVES 4

2 eggplants, thinly sliced lengthwise
5 tbsp olive oil
1 garlic clove, crushed
4 tbsp pesto

1½ cups grated mozzarella cheese
small bunch fresh basil leaves, torn, plus extra
   sprigs to garnish
salt and pepper

1. Preheat the oven to 350°F/180°C. Sprinkle the eggplant slices liberally with salt and let stand for 10–15 minutes to extract the bitter juices. Turn the slices over and repeat. Rinse well with cold water and drain on paper towels.

2. Heat the oil in a large skillet and add the garlic. Fry the eggplant slices lightly on both sides, a few at a time. Drain on paper towels.

3. Spread the pesto onto one side of the eggplant slices. Top with the mozzarella and sprinkle with the torn basil leaves. Season with a little salt and pepper. Roll up the slices and secure with wooden toothpicks.

4. Arrange the eggplant rolls in an ovenproof baking dish. Place in the preheated oven and bake for 8–10 minutes.

5. Transfer the eggplant rolls to a warmed serving plate. Garnish with basil sprigs and serve immediately.

Marinated Mushrooms

SERVES 6–8

2 lb 4 oz/1 kg mixed exotic mushrooms,
    such as porcini, chanterelles, oyster, and/
    or cremini
1 fresh red chile

1 cup olive oil
½ cup white balsamic vinegar
fresh rosemary or oregano sprigs
salt

1. Wipe the mushrooms with damp paper towels. Cut the chile in half lengthwise, remove the seeds, and cut into thin strips. Set aside.

2. Heat 5 tablespoons of the oil in a large saucepan, then add the mushrooms and cook, stirring, until all the juices have evaporated. Add the reserved chile strips and cook, stirring, for an additional 1–2 minutes. Stir in the vinegar and season to taste with salt.

3. Tip the contents of the saucepan into a bowl, then stir in the rosemary sprigs and pour over the remaining oil. Cover with plastic wrap and let marinate in the refrigerator overnight before serving.

Marinated White Beans

1¼ cups dried cannellini beans
1 bay leaf
1 garlic clove
4 scallions
1 tbsp lemon juice

3 tbsp white wine vinegar
5 tbsp olive oil
salt and pepper
chopped fresh parsley and fresh Parmesan
cheese shavings, to serve

1. Place the beans in a large bowl, cover with plenty of water, and let soak overnight.

2. Pour the beans with their soaking water into a saucepan, add the bay leaf and whole garlic clove, and bring to a boil. Reduce the heat and simmer gently, occasionally skimming off any foam, for 1–1½ hours, or until the beans are tender.

3. Remove from the heat and discard the bay leaf and garlic. Let the beans cool in the cooking water until lukewarm. Meanwhile, cut the scallions into thin strips and set aside. Mix the lemon juice, vinegar, and oil in a bowl with salt and pepper to taste to make a dressing.

4. Strain the beans through a colander and drain well. Transfer to a large serving bowl, stir in the scallions and dressing, and let steep for at least 15 minutes. Scatter over the parsley and Parmesan cheese shavings just before serving.

Sun-Dried Tomato Bagna Calda with Spring Vegetables

SERVES 4

1 lb 12 oz/800 g prepared mixed spring
vegetables, such as celery stalks, asparagus
spears, broccoli florets, and artichoke hearts

country-style bread, cut into bite-size cubes,
toasted if preferred

BAGNA CALDA

generous ¾ cup extra virgin olive oil

3 garlic cloves, thinly sliced

1¾ oz/50 g canned anchovy fillets, drained

1 tbsp unsalted butter (optional)

3–4 sun-dried tomatoes in oil, drained and very
finely chopped

4–5 fresh basil leaves, torn

1. Lightly cook the vegetables, if you want, in separate pans of boiling water until just tender. Drain
    and let cool.

2. Arrange all the vegetables on a serving plate with the bread cubes. Alternatively, serve the bread
    cubes in a separate little basket or dish.

3. To make the bagna calda, put the oil, garlic, and anchovies in a saucepan over low heat. Mash
    the anchovies with a fork and heat, stirring, for 3–4 minutes, or until they have started to melt
    into the oil and the garlic slices have softened. Be careful to avoid letting the mixture become
    too hot, or the garlic will simply fry and the mixture will be ruined. Stir in the butter, if using,
    and sun-dried tomatoes.

4. Transfer the mixture to a small serving bowl and stir in the basil. Serve immediately with the
    prepared vegetables and bread cubes.

Mixed Antipasto Meat Platter

SERVES 4

1 cantaloupe melon
2 oz/55 g Italian salami, thinly sliced
8 slices prosciutto
8 slices bresaola
8 slices mortadella
4 plum tomatoes, thinly sliced
4 fresh figs, halved

⅔ cup black olives, pitted
2 tbsp fresh oregano leaves
4 tbsp extra virgin olive oil, plus extra
   to serve
pepper
ciabatta, to serve

1. Cut the melon in half, scoop out and discard the seeds, then cut the flesh into 8 wedges. Arrange the wedges on one end of a large serving platter.

2. Arrange the salami, prosciutto, bresaola, and mortadella in loose folds on the other end of the platter. Arrange the tomato slices and fig halves along the center of the platter.

3. Sprinkle the olives and oregano over the platter and drizzle with oil. Season to taste with pepper, then serve with ciabatta and extra oil for dipping and drizzling.

Beef Carpaccio

SERVES 4

7 oz/200 g beef tenderloin, in one piece
2 tbsp lemon juice
4 tbsp extra virgin olive oil
½ cup Parmesan cheese shavings

4 tbsp chopped fresh flat-leaf parsley
salt and pepper
lemon wedges, to garnish
fresh bread, to serve

1. Using a sharp knife, cut the beef into paper-thin slices and arrange on 4 individual serving plates.

2. Pour the lemon juice into a small bowl and season to taste with salt and pepper. Stir in the oil, then pour the dressing over the meat. Cover the plates with plastic wrap and set aside for 10–15 minutes to marinate.

3. Remove and discard the plastic wrap. Arrange the Parmesan shavings in the center of each serving and sprinkle with parsley. Garnish with lemon wedges and serve with fresh bread.

Pan-Fried Shrimp

SERVES 4

4 garlic cloves
20–24 large shrimp, deveined
8 tbsp butter
4 tbsp olive oil

6 tbsp brandy
salt and pepper
chopped fresh parsley, to garnish
lemon wedges, to serve

1. Using a sharp knife, peel and slice the garlic. Wash the shrimp and pat dry using paper towels.

2. Melt the butter with the oil in a large skillet, add the garlic and shrimp, and fry over high heat, stirring, for 3–4 minutes, until the shrimp are pink.

3. Sprinkle with brandy and season to taste with salt and pepper. Sprinkle with parsley and serve immediately with lemon wedges for squeezing over.

Pan-Fried Whole Sardines

SERVES 4

1 lb 2 oz/500 g small fresh sardines, scaled

all-purpose flour, for dusting

olive oil, for shallow-frying

coarse sea salt and lemon wedges, to serve

1. Wash the sardines and pat dry with paper towels. If the sardines are longer than 3½ inches/9 cm, remove the heads and gut them. Smaller fish may be cooked whole.

2. Spread out the flour on a plate and use to coat the sardines, tapping off any excess.

3. Heat a depth of 1½ inches/4 cm of oil in a skillet and cook the sardines over medium–high heat until golden brown. Transfer to a serving plate, sprinkle with sea salt, and serve with lemon wedges for squeezing over.

Vegetable Soup with Pesto

SERVES 6

1 tbsp olive oil

1 onion, finely chopped

1 large leek, thinly sliced

1 celery stalk, thinly sliced

1 carrot, quartered and thinly sliced

1 garlic clove, finely chopped

6¼ cups water

1 potato, diced

1 parsnip, finely diced

1 small kohlrabi or turnip, diced

5½ oz/150 g green beans, cut into small pieces

1⅓ cups fresh or frozen peas

2 small zucchini, quartered lengthwise and sliced

14 oz/400 g canned cannellini beans, drained and rinsed

3½ oz/100 g spinach leaves, cut into thin ribbons

salt and pepper

PESTO

1 large garlic clove, very finely chopped

½ cup fresh basil leaves, plus extra sprigs to garnish

1 cup grated Parmesan cheese

4 tbsp extra virgin olive oil

1. Heat the olive oil in a large saucepan over low–medium heat. Add the onion and leek and cook for 5 minutes, stirring occasionally, until the onion has softened. Add the celery, carrot, and garlic and cook, covered, for an additional 5 minutes, stirring frequently.

2. Add the water, potato, parsnip, kohlrabi, and green beans. Bring to a boil, reduce the heat to low, and simmer, covered, for 5 minutes.

3. Add the peas, zucchini, and cannellini beans and season generously with salt and pepper. Cover again and simmer for about 25 minutes, until all the vegetables are tender.

4. Meanwhile, make the pesto. Put the garlic, basil, and Parmesan in a food processor with the extra virgin olive oil and process until smooth, scraping down the sides as necessary. Alternatively, pound together using a mortar and pestle.

5. Add the spinach to the soup and simmer for an additional 5 minutes. Taste and adjust the seasoning, adding salt and pepper if needed, and stir about a tablespoon of the pesto into the soup. Ladle into warmed bowls, garnish with basil sprigs, and serve with the remaining pesto.

Bread and Tomato Soup

SERVES 6

1 lb/450 g two-day-old crusty Italian open-
textured bread, such as Pugliese

2 lb 4 oz/1 kg ripe plum tomatoes

4 tbsp olive oil

4 garlic cloves, crushed

scant 2½ cups boiling water

1 bunch of fresh basil

salt and pepper

extra virgin olive oil, to serve

1. Cut the bread into slices and then cubes (you can remove some of the crusts if you want) and let dry
    out for 30 minutes. Meanwhile, peel the tomatoes and cut into chunks.

2. Heat the olive oil in a large pan, then add the garlic and cook over medium heat, stirring, for
    1 minute without browning. Add the tomatoes and simmer gently for 20–30 minutes, or until the
    mixture has thickened.

3. Add the bread and stir until it has absorbed the liquid. Stir in the boiling water until you have a
    thick soupy mixture. Season to taste with salt and pepper.

4. Remove the basil leaves from their stems and tear any large leaves into pieces. Stir the basil into
    the soup.

5. Serve the soup warm, drizzled with extra virgin olive oil.

Ribollita

SERVES 4

3 tbsp olive oil

2 red onions, coarsely chopped

3 carrots, sliced

3 celery stalks, coarsely chopped

3 garlic cloves, chopped

1 tbsp chopped fresh thyme

14 oz/400 g canned cannellini beans, drained and rinsed

14 oz/400 g canned chopped tomatoes

2½ cups water or vegetable stock

2 tbsp chopped fresh parsley

1 lb 2 oz/500 g Tuscan kale or savoy cabbage, trimmed and sliced

1 small day-old ciabatta loaf, torn into small pieces

salt and pepper

extra virgin olive oil, to serve

1. Heat the olive oil in a large saucepan and cook the onions, carrots, and celery for 10–15 minutes, stirring frequently. Add the garlic, thyme, and salt and pepper to taste. Continue to cook for an additional 1–2 minutes, until the vegetables are golden and caramelized.

2. Add the beans to the pan and pour in the tomatoes. Add enough of the water to cover the vegetables. Bring to a boil and simmer for 20 minutes. Add the parsley and Tuscan kale and cook for an additional 5 minutes.

3. Stir in the bread and add a little more water, if needed. The soup should be thick.

4. Taste and adjust the seasoning, adding salt and pepper if needed. Ladle into warmed serving bowls and serve hot, drizzled with extra virgin olive oil.

Tuscan Bean Soup

SERVES 6

10½ oz/300 g canned cannellini beans, drained
 and rinsed

10½ oz/300 g canned cranberry beans, drained
 and rinsed

2½ cups chicken or vegetable stock

4 oz/115 g dried conchigliette or other small
 pasta shapes

4 tbsp olive oil

2 garlic cloves, finely chopped

3 tbsp chopped fresh flat-leaf parsley

salt and pepper

1. Place half the cannellini and half the cranberry beans in a food processor with half the stock and process until smooth. Pour into a large, heavy-bottom pan and add the remaining beans. Stir in enough of the remaining stock to achieve the consistency you like, then bring to a boil.

2. Add the pasta and return to a boil, then reduce the heat and cook for 15 minutes, or until tender.

3. Meanwhile, heat 3 tablespoons of the oil in a small skillet. Add the garlic and cook, stirring constantly, for 2–3 minutes, or until golden. Stir the garlic into the soup with the parsley.

4. Season to taste with salt and pepper and ladle into warmed soup bowls. Drizzle with the remaining oil and serve immediately.

First Course

The first course (*primo piatto*) of an Italian meal usually comprises a grain-based dish: pasta, gnocchi, risotto, or polenta. Pasta is universally popular and is easy to cook and wonderfully versatile. It is served in soups, with a variety of sauces, or stuffed and baked in the oven. Some of the best-known pasta dishes are made with long strands or ribbons combined with a hearty sauce. Spaghetti Bolognese and Spaghetti alla Carbonara are well-known classics, but there are other sauces worth trying—fiery tomato-based *arrabbiata,* for example, or the robust *puttanesca* with tomatoes, capers, olives, and anchovies. Delicately stuffed ravioli squares with a simple herb butter sauce are also good as a first course, as are Spinach Cannelloni or Lasagna al Forno.

Gnocchi are feather-light, tiny dumplings made with mashed potatoes and flour, or flour on its own, often flavored with spinach or some kind

of cheese. They are cooked in boiling water and served with various sauces or simply topped with cheese and butter.

All types of risotto are served as a first course, particularly in northern Italy, where rice is a major crop. Risotto is made with short-grain rice, which is characteristically creamier than long-grain rice. Parmesan is a key ingredient in risotto, except those containing fish or seafood, and is stirred in just before serving.

Polenta is also popular in northern Italy. It is made with cornmeal and water, and is served either as a soft porridge or a firmer cake that is fried, baked, or broiled until crisp. In the north-central region, polenta is usually served soft and creamy, often mixed with cheese. Further east you are more likely to find it fried or broiled.

Spaghetti Bolognese

SERVES 4

1 tbsp olive oil

1 onion, finely chopped

2 garlic cloves, chopped

1 carrot, chopped

1 celery stalk, chopped

1¾ oz/50 g pancetta or bacon, diced

12 oz/350 g lean ground beef

14 oz/400 g canned chopped tomatoes

2 tsp dried oregano

½ cup red wine

2 tbsp tomato paste

12 oz/350 g dried spaghetti

salt and pepper

fresh Parmesan cheese shavings, to serve

1. Heat the oil in a large skillet. Add the onion and cook for 3 minutes, until softened. Add the garlic, carrot, celery, and pancetta and sauté for 3–4 minutes, or until just beginning to brown.

2. Add the beef and cook over high heat for an additional 3 minutes, or until all of the meat is browned. Stir in the tomatoes, oregano, and red wine and bring to a boil. Reduce the heat and simmer for about 45 minutes. Stir in the tomato paste and season to taste with salt and pepper.

3. Meanwhile, bring a large saucepan of lightly salted water to a boil. Add the spaghetti, bring back to a boil, and cook for 8–10 minutes, or until tender but still firm to the bite. Drain thoroughly.

4. Transfer the spaghetti to a serving plate and pour over the bolognese sauce. Toss to mix well and serve with Parmesan cheese shavings.

Spaghetti alla Carbonara

SERVES 4

14 oz/400 g dried spaghetti
4 eggs
4 tbsp heavy cream
½ cup grated Parmesan cheese

½ cup grated pecorino cheese
1 tbsp butter
150 g/5½ oz pancetta, diced
salt and pepper

1. Bring a large saucepan of lightly salted water to a boil. Add the pasta, bring back to a boil, and cook for 8–10 minutes, or until tender but still firm to the bite.

2. Meanwhile, beat the eggs in a bowl with the cream, cheeses, and salt and pepper to taste. Melt the butter in a large, deep skillet and fry the pancetta until crispy.

3. Drain the pasta, but not too thoroughly, then add to the skillet and pour over the egg mixture. Remove from the heat and stir until the egg mixture is warmed through but still creamy.

4. Transfer to warmed serving plates and sprinkle with freshly ground black pepper. Serve immediately.

Pasta Arrabbiata

SERVES 4

⅔ cup dry white wine

1 tbsp sun-dried tomato paste

2 fresh red chiles

2 garlic cloves, finely chopped

12 oz/350 g dried tortiglioni

4 tbsp chopped fresh flat-leaf parsley

salt and pepper

fresh pecorino cheese shavings, to garnish

SUGOCASA

5 tbsp extra virgin olive oil

1 lb/450 g plum tomatoes, chopped

salt and pepper

1. To make the sugocasa, heat the oil in a skillet over high heat until almost smoking. Add the tomatoes and cook, stirring frequently, for 2-3 minutes. Reduce the heat to low and cook gently for 20 minutes, or until soft. Season to taste with salt and pepper. Using a wooden spoon, press through a nonmetallic strainer into a saucepan.

2. Add the wine, sun-dried tomato paste, whole chiles, and garlic to the sugocasa and bring to a boil. Reduce the heat and simmer gently.

3. Meanwhile, bring a large saucepan of lightly salted water to a boil. Add the pasta, return to a boil, and cook for 8–10 minutes, or until tender but still firm to the bite.

4. Remove the chiles and taste the sauce. If you prefer a hotter flavor, chop some or all of the chiles and return to the pan. Check and adjust the seasoning, adding salt and pepper if needed, then stir in half the parsley.

5. Drain the pasta and transfer to a warmed serving bowl. Add the sauce and toss to coat. Sprinkle with the remaining parsley, garnish with the pecorino cheese shavings, and serve immediately.

Tagliatelle with Basil Pesto

SERVES 4

1 lb/450 g dried tagliatelle
salt

BASIL PESTO
2 garlic cloves
¼ cup pine nuts
2½ cups fresh basil leaves, plus extra
   to garnish
½ cup olive oil
½ cup freshly grated Parmesan cheese
salt

1. To make the basil pesto, put the garlic and pine nuts into a food processor or blender and process briefly. Add the basil leaves and process to a paste. With the motor still running, gradually add the oil. Scrape into a bowl and beat in the Parmesan cheese. Season to taste with salt. Alternatively, pound together using a mortar and pestle.

2. Bring a large saucepan of lightly salted water to a boil. Add the pasta, return to a boil, and cook for 8–10 minutes, or until tender but still firm to the bite.

3. Drain the pasta well, return to the saucepan, and toss with half the pesto. Divide among warmed serving plates and top with the remaining pesto. Garnish with basil and serve immediately.

Spaghetti alla Norma

SERVES 4

¾ cup olive oil

1 lb 2 oz/500 g plum tomatoes, peeled and chopped

1 garlic clove, chopped

12 oz/350 g eggplants, diced

14 oz/400 g dried spaghetti

½ bunch fresh basil, torn

1⅓ cups grated pecorino cheese

salt and pepper

1. Heat 4 tablespoons of the oil in a large pan. Add the tomatoes and garlic, season to taste with salt and pepper, cover, and cook over low heat, stirring occasionally, for 25 minutes.

2. Meanwhile, heat the remaining oil in a heavy skillet. Add the eggplants and cook, stirring occasionally, for 5 minutes, until evenly golden brown. Remove with a slotted spoon and drain on paper towels.

3. Bring a large pan of lightly salted water to a boil. Add the pasta, bring back to a boil, and cook for 8–10 minutes, or until tender but still firm to the bite.

4. Meanwhile, stir the drained eggplants into the tomato mixture. Taste and adjust the seasoning, adding salt and pepper if needed.

5. Drain the pasta and place in a warmed serving dish. Add the tomato-and-eggplant mixture, basil, and half the pecorino cheese. Toss well, sprinkle with the remaining cheese, and serve immediately.

Spaghetti alla Puttanesca

SERVES 4

3 tbsp olive oil

2 garlic cloves, finely chopped

10 canned anchovy fillets, drained and
  chopped

1 cup black olives, pitted and chopped

1 tbsp capers, drained and rinsed

1 lb/450 g plum tomatoes, peeled, seeded, and
  chopped

pinch of cayenne pepper

14 oz/400 g dried spaghetti

salt

2 tbsp chopped fresh parsley, to garnish
  (optional)

1. Heat the oil in a heavy-bottom skillet. Add the garlic and cook over low heat, stirring frequently, for 2 minutes. Add the anchovies and mash them to a pulp with a fork. Add the olives, capers, and tomatoes and season to taste with cayenne pepper. Cover and simmer for 25 minutes.

2. Meanwhile, bring a large, heavy-bottom pan of lightly salted water to a boil. Add the pasta, return to a boil, and cook for 8–10 minutes, or until tender but still firm to the bite. Drain well and transfer to a warmed serving dish.

3. Spoon the anchovy sauce into the dish and toss the pasta, using 2 large forks. Garnish with the chopped parsley, if using, and serve immediately.

Spaghetti con Vongole

SERVES 4

2 lb 4 oz/1 kg clams, scrubbed
¾ cup water
¾ cup dry white wine
12 oz/350 g dried spaghetti

5 tbsp olive oil
2 garlic cloves, finely chopped
4 tbsp chopped fresh flat-leaf parsley
salt and pepper

1 Discard any clams with broken shells and any that refuse to close when tapped. Place the clams in a large, heavy-bottom pan. Add the water and wine, then cover and cook over high heat, shaking the pan occasionally, for 5 minutes, or until the shells have opened. Remove the clams with a slotted spoon and strain the liquid through a cheesecloth-lined strainer into a small pan. Bring to a boil and cook until reduced by about half. Discard any clams that remain closed and remove the remainder from their shells.

2. Bring a large, heavy-bottom pan of lightly salted water to a boil. Add the pasta, return to a boil, and cook for 8–10 minutes, or until tender but still firm to the bite.

3. Meanwhile, heat the oil in a large, heavy-bottom skillet. Add the garlic and cook, stirring frequently, for 2 minutes. Add the parsley and the reduced cooking liquid and simmer gently. Drain the pasta and add it to the skillet with the clams. Season to taste with salt and pepper and cook, stirring constantly, for 4 minutes, or until the pasta is coated and the clams have heated through. Transfer to a warmed serving dish and serve immediately.

Sweet Potato Ravioli with Sage Butter

SERVES 4

PASTA

generous 2¾ cups type "00" pasta flour or
    all-purpose flour

4 eggs, beaten

semolina, for dusting

salt

FILLING

1 lb 2 oz/500 g sweet potatoes

3 tbsp olive oil

1 large onion, finely chopped

1 garlic clove, crushed

1 tsp chopped fresh thyme leaves

2 tbsp honey

salt and pepper

SAGE BUTTER

4 tbsp butter

1 bunch fresh sage leaves, finely chopped,
    reserving a few leaves to garnish

1. To make the pasta, sift the flour into a large bowl or food processor. Add the eggs and bring the mixture together or process to make a soft but not sticky dough. Turn out onto a counter lightly dusted with semolina and knead for 4–5 minutes, or until smooth. Cover with plastic wrap and let chill in the refrigerator for at least 30 minutes.

2. For the filling, peel the sweet potatoes and cut into chunks. Cook in a saucepan of boiling water for 20 minutes, or until tender. Drain and mash. Heat the oil in a skillet over medium heat, then add the onion and cook, stirring frequently, for 4–5 minutes, or until softened but not colored. Stir the onion into the mashed potatoes and add the garlic and thyme. Drizzle with the honey and season to taste with salt and pepper. Set aside.

3. Using a pasta machine or rolling pin, roll the pasta out to a thickness of about 1⁄32 inch/1 mm. Cut the pasta in half. Place teaspoonfuls of the filling at evenly spaced intervals across one half of the pasta. Brush around the filling with a little water and cover with the second half of pasta. Press lightly around the filling to seal the pasta and cut into squares with a sharp knife or pastry wheel. Lay the ravioli out on a sheet of wax paper that has been lightly dusted with semolina.

4. Bring a large saucepan of salted water to a boil and drop in the ravioli. Cook for 2–3 minutes, until the pasta rises to the surface and is tender but still firm to the bite.

5. Meanwhile, for the sage butter, melt the butter with the sage in a small saucepan over low heat.

6. Drain the ravioli and toss with the sage butter. Serve immediately, garnished with sage leaves.

Lasagna al Forno

SERVES 4

2 tbsp olive oil

2 oz/55 g pancetta, chopped

1 onion, chopped

1 garlic clove, finely chopped

8 oz/225 g ground beef

2 celery stalks, chopped

2 carrots, chopped

pinch of sugar

½ tsp dried oregano

14 oz/400 g canned chopped tomatoes

8 oz/225 g dried lasagna sheets

1 cup grated Parmesan cheese, plus extra
   for sprinkling

salt and pepper

CHEESE SAUCE

2 tbsp butter

¼ cup all-purpose flour

1¼ cups warm milk

scant 1¼ cups grated cheddar cheese

2 tsp Dijon mustard

salt and pepper

1. Preheat the oven to 375°F/190°C. Heat the oil in a large, heavy-bottom pan. Add the pancetta and cook over medium heat, stirring occasionally, for 3 minutes, or until the fat starts to run. Add the onion and garlic and cook, stirring occasionally, for 5 minutes, or until softened.

2. Add the beef and cook, breaking it up with a wooden spoon, until browned all over. Stir in the celery and carrots and cook for 5 minutes. Season to taste with salt and pepper. Add the sugar, oregano, and tomatoes and their can juices. Bring to a boil, reduce the heat, and simmer for 30 minutes.

3. Meanwhile, bring a large pan of lightly salted water to a boil. Add the lasagna sheets, bring back to a boil, and cook for 8–10 minutes, or according to the package directions. Drain well.

4. To make the cheese sauce, melt the butter in a pan. Add the flour and cook over low heat, stirring constantly, for 2 minutes. Remove the pan from the heat and gradually stir in the milk. Return the pan to low heat and bring to a boil, stirring constantly. Simmer, stirring constantly, until thickened and smooth. Stir in the cheddar cheese until it melts and add the mustard. Season to taste with salt and pepper.

5. In a large, rectangular ovenproof dish, make alternate layers of meat sauce, lasagna sheets, and half the Parmesan cheese. Pour the cheese sauce over the layers, covering them completely, and sprinkle with the remaining Parmesan cheese. Bake in the preheated oven for 30 minutes, or until golden brown and bubbling. Serve immediately, sprinkled with extra Parmesan cheese.

Spinach Cannelloni

SERVES 4

oil, for greasing
12 dried cannelloni tubes
1 lb 5 oz/600 g spinach
2 tbsp butter
1 small onion, finely chopped
1 cup ricotta cheese
½ tsp freshly grated nutmeg
½ cup grated Parmesan cheese
salt and pepper

BÉCHAMEL SAUCE
2½ cups milk
1 bay leaf
6 black peppercorns
slice of onion
blade of mace
4 tbsp butter
½ cup all-purpose flour
salt and pepper

1. Preheat the oven to 400°F/200°C. Oil a large, rectangular baking dish. Cook the cannelloni in a large pan of lightly salted water for 8–10 minutes, or according to the package directions. Drain well.

2. To make the béchamel sauce, pour the milk into a pan and add the bay leaf, peppercorns, onion, and mace. Bring to just below boiling point, then remove from the heat and let steep for 10 minutes. Strain the milk into a pitcher, discarding the seasonings. Melt the butter in a separate pan. Add the flour and cook over low heat, stirring constantly, for 2 minutes. Remove the pan from the heat and gradually stir in the flavored milk. Return the pan to low heat and bring to a boil, stirring constantly. Simmer, stirring constantly, until thickened and smooth. Season to taste with salt and pepper.

3. Remove and discard any tough stems from the spinach, then place the leaves in a colander and wash under cold running water. Let drain.

4. Melt the butter in a large saucepan over medium heat and cook the onion for 4–5 minutes, until softened and translucent. Stir in the spinach, with the water still clinging to its leaves, cover, and cook for an additional 3–4 minutes, until wilted.

5. Transfer the spinach-and-onion mixture to a strainer and let drain, then squeeze out as much water as possible. Finely chop the spinach, then transfer to a bowl with the ricotta cheese, nutmeg, and salt and pepper to taste. Mix well and set aside.

6. Spoon the spinach mixture into a pastry bag fitted with a large, plain tip and use to fill the cannelloni tubes. Place the filled cannelloni tubes in the prepared baking dish, pour over the béchamel sauce, and sprinkle with the Parmesan cheese. Bake in the preheated oven for 25–30 minutes. Serve immediately.

Potato Gnocchi with Walnut Pesto

SERVES 4

1 lb/450 g starchy potatoes
½ cup grated Parmesan cheese
1 egg, beaten
scant 1½ cups all-purpose flour, plus extra for
    dusting
salt and pepper

WALNUT PESTO
1½ oz/40 g fresh flat-leaf parsley
2 tbsp capers, rinsed
2 garlic cloves
¾ cup extra virgin olive oil
scant ¾ cup walnut halves
⅓ cup grated pecorino or Parmesan cheese
salt and pepper

1. Boil the potatoes in their skins in a large pan of water for 30–35 minutes, or until tender. Drain well
    and let cool slightly.

2. Meanwhile, to make the walnut pesto, chop the parsley, capers, and garlic, then put in a mortar
    with the oil, walnuts, and salt and pepper to taste. Pound with a pestle to a coarse paste. Add the
    pecorino cheese and stir well.

3. When the potatoes are cool enough to handle, peel off the skins and pass the flesh through a
    strainer into a large bowl or press through a potato ricer. While still hot, season well with salt and
    pepper and add the Parmesan cheese. Beat in the egg and sift in the flour. Lightly mix together,
    then turn out onto a lightly floured counter. Knead lightly until the mixture becomes a smooth
    dough. If it is too sticky, add a little more flour.

4. Roll the dough out on a lightly floured counter with your hands into a long log. Cut into
    1-inch/2.5-cm pieces and gently press with a fork to give the traditional ridged effect. Transfer
    to a floured cookie sheet and cover with a clean dish towel while you make the remaining gnocchi.

5. Bring a large pan of water to a boil, then add the gnocchi, in small batches, and cook for
    1–2 minutes. Remove with a slotted spoon and transfer to a warmed serving dish to keep
    warm while you cook the remaining gnocchi.

6. Serve the gnocchi in warmed serving bowls with a good spoonful of the pesto on top.

Spinach and Ricotta Gnocchi

SERVES 4–6

1 tbsp olive oil

1 lb 2 oz/500 g spinach leaves

1 cup ricotta cheese

1 cup grated Parmesan or pecorino cheese

2 eggs, lightly beaten

generous ⅓ cup all-purpose flour, plus extra for dusting

freshly grated nutmeg

salt and pepper

SAUCE

2 tbsp olive oil

2 shallots, finely chopped

1 carrot, finely diced

2 garlic cloves, crushed

1 lb 12 oz/800 g canned chopped tomatoes

1 tbsp tomato paste

6 fresh basil leaves, coarsely torn into pieces, plus extra to garnish

salt and pepper

1. Heat the oil in a large saucepan. Add the spinach and cook, covered, for 1–2 minutes, or until just wilted. Drain through a colander and let cool, then squeeze out as much water as possible.

2. Finely chop the spinach and put in a bowl. Add the ricotta cheese, half the Parmesan cheese, the eggs, and flour and mix well. Season to taste with salt, pepper, and nutmeg. Cover and let chill in the refrigerator for at least 1 hour.

3. Meanwhile, make the sauce. Heat the oil in a saucepan, then add the shallots, carrot, and garlic and cook over medium heat, stirring frequently, for 3–4 minutes, or until softened. Add the tomatoes and tomato paste and bring to a boil, then reduce the heat and simmer, uncovered, for 10–15 minutes, or until the sauce is reduced and thickened. Season to taste with salt and pepper and add the basil. If you like a smooth sauce, pass it through a strainer or process in a food processor or blender.

4. To shape the gnocchi, flour a plate and your hands thoroughly. Put a dessertspoonful of the spinach mixture into the palm of one hand, then roll gently into an egg shape and transfer to a floured cookie sheet. Repeat with the remaining spinach mixture.

5. Bring a large saucepan of water to a simmer. Carefully add the gnocchi, in small batches, and cook gently for 2–3 minutes, or until they rise to the surface. Remove with a slotted spoon and transfer to a warmed serving dish to keep warm while you cook the remaining gnocchi.

6. Transfer the gnocchi to individual serving dishes and top with the sauce. Sprinkle over the remaining Parmesan cheese, garnish with basil, and serve immediately.

Baked Polenta with Cheese and Thyme

SERVES 4

2½ cups water

2½ cups milk

1 tsp sea salt

½ tsp freshly grated nutmeg

2 cups fine cornmeal

¼ cup finely grated Parmesan cheese

scant 1¼ cups raclette or Mahon cheese, cubed

4 tbsp unsalted butter, plus extra
  for greasing

2 fresh thyme sprigs, leaves only

pepper

salad greens, to serve

1. Put the water and milk in a large pan and bring to a boil over high heat. Add the salt, pepper to taste, and nutmeg, then pour in the cornmeal, stirring constantly. Reduce the heat to medium and cook, stirring constantly, for an additional 25–30 minutes, or until thick and pulling away from the sides of the pan.

2. Remove from the heat and add the Parmesan cheese and half the raclette cheese and butter. Stir until melted and well combined.

3. Pour the polenta onto a cold, nonstick baking sheet, then spread out to a thickness of ½ inch/1 cm and let cool completely.

4. Meanwhile, preheat the oven to 400°F/200°C. Grease a shallow baking dish. Using a plain cookie cutter, cut out 2-inch/5-cm circles and arrange, overlapping, in the prepared baking dish.

5. Dice the remaining butter and cheese, then scatter over the polenta with the thyme leaves.

6. Bake in the preheated oven for 15 minutes, or until golden and crisp. Serve with salad greens.

Risotto Primavera

SERVES 4

6½ cups chicken or vegetable stock

8 oz/225 g fine asparagus spears

4 tbsp olive oil

6 oz/175 g young green beans, cut into
1-inch/2.5-cm lengths

6 oz/175 g young zucchini, quartered and cut
into 1-inch/2.5-cm lengths

generous 1½ cups shelled fresh peas

1 onion, finely chopped

1–2 garlic cloves, finely chopped

generous 1½ cups risotto rice

4 scallions, cut into 1-inch/2.5-cm lengths

4 tbsp butter

1 cup grated Parmesan cheese

2 tbsp snipped fresh chives

2 tbsp shredded fresh basil

salt and pepper

1. Bring the stock to a boil in a pan, then reduce the heat and keep simmering gently over low heat
   while you are cooking the risotto.

2. Trim the woody ends of the asparagus and cut off the tips. Cut the stems into 1-inch/2.5-cm pieces
   and set aside with the tips.

3. Heat 2 tablespoons of the oil in a large skillet over high heat until hot. Add the asparagus, beans,
   zucchini, and peas and stir-fry for 3–4 minutes, until they are bright green and just starting to soften.
   Set aside.

4. Heat the remaining oil in a large, heavy-bottom pan over medium heat. Add the onion and cook,
   stirring occasionally, for 3 minutes, or until it starts to soften. Stir in the garlic and cook, while
   stirring, for 30 seconds.

5. Reduce the heat, add the rice, and mix to coat in oil. Cook, stirring constantly, for 2–3 minutes,
   or until the grains are translucent.

6. Gradually add the hot stock, a ladleful at a time. Stir constantly and add more liquid as the
   rice absorbs each addition. Cook for 20 minutes, or until all but 2 tablespoons of the liquid has
   been absorbed and the rice is creamy but still firm to the bite.

7. Stir in the stir-fried vegetables and scallions with the remaining stock. Cook for 2 minutes, stirring
   frequently, then season to taste with salt and pepper. Stir in the butter, Parmesan cheese, chives,
   and basil. Remove the pan from the heat. Transfer the risotto to warmed serving dishes and serve
   immediately.

Mushroom Risotto

SERVES 4

2 oz/55 g dried porcini

generous 1 cup warm water

scant 3 cups chicken stock

6 tbsp olive oil

10 oz/280 g mixed fresh wild or portobello
  mushrooms, thickly sliced

2 garlic cloves, finely chopped

1 tbsp finely chopped fresh thyme

1 onion, finely chopped

generous 1½ cups risotto rice

⅔ cup dry white wine

4 tbsp butter

1 cup grated Parmesan cheese

salt and pepper

2 tbsp finely chopped fresh flat-leaf parsley,
  to garnish

1. Soak the dried mushrooms in the warm water in a small bowl for 10–15 minutes. Drain, reserving the soaking liquid (strain it thoroughly to remove any grit). Finely slice the drained mushrooms.

2. Bring the stock to a boil in a pan, then reduce the heat and keep simmering gently over low heat while you are cooking the risotto.

3. Heat half the oil in a large skillet, then add the fresh mushrooms and cook over low heat, stirring occasionally, for 10–15 minutes, or until softened. Add the soaked dried mushrooms and garlic and cook, stirring frequently, for an additional 2–3 minutes. Add the thyme and salt and pepper to taste, then remove the mushroom mixture from the skillet and keep warm.

4. Heat the remaining oil in the skillet, then add the onion and cook over low heat, stirring occasionally, for 10–12 minutes, or until softened. Gently stir in the rice and cook, stirring, for 1 minute. Pour in the wine and cook, stirring, until it has all been absorbed. Add the reserved mushroom soaking liquid and cook, stirring, until it has all been absorbed.

5. Gradually add the hot stock, a ladleful at a time. Stir constantly and add more liquid as the rice absorbs each addition. Cook for 20 minutes, or until all the liquid has been absorbed and the rice is creamy but still firm to the bite.

6. Remove from the heat and gently stir in the mushroom mixture, butter, and half the Parmesan cheese. Season to taste with salt and pepper.

7. Serve immediately on warmed plates, sprinkled with the parsley and the remaining cheese.

Sage and Gorgonzola Risotto

SERVES 4

4 cups chicken or vegetable stock

4 tbsp unsalted butter

5½ oz/150 g pancetta, cubed

1 small onion, chopped

2 garlic cloves, crushed

scant 1½ cups risotto rice

½ cup white wine or vermouth

generous 1½ cups Gorgonzola cheese, crumbled

2 tbsp finely chopped fresh sage, plus extra leaves to garnish

2 tbsp finely grated Parmesan cheese

salt and pepper

1. Bring the stock to a boil in a pan, then reduce the heat and keep simmering gently over low heat while you are cooking the risotto.

2. Heat half the butter in a large pan or skillet and cook the pancetta over medium–high heat, stirring frequently, until the fat melts and the pancetta is beginning to brown. Add the onion and garlic and cook, stirring frequently, for 5 minutes, or until the onion has softened.

3. Add the rice and stir to coat in the pancetta mixture. Pour in the wine and cook, stirring constantly, until almost all the liquid has been absorbed.

4. Gradually add the hot stock, a ladleful at a time. Stir constantly and add more liquid as the rice absorbs each addition. Cook for 20 minutes, or until all the liquid has been absorbed and the rice is creamy but still firm to the bite.

5. Remove from the heat, then add the Gorgonzola cheese and chopped sage and stir until the cheese has melted. Season to taste with salt and pepper, then add the remaining butter and the Parmesan cheese. Serve immediately, garnished with sage leaves.

Chicken Risotto with Saffron

SERVES 6–8

generous 5½ cups chicken stock

generous ½ cup butter

2 lb/900 g skinless, boneless chicken breasts,
  thinly sliced

1 large onion, chopped

generous 2¼ cups risotto rice

⅔ cup white wine

1 tsp crumbled saffron threads

½ cup grated Parmesan cheese

salt and pepper

1. Bring the stock to a boil in a pan, then reduce the heat and keep simmering gently over low heat while you are cooking the risotto.

2. Meanwhile, heat 4 tablespoons of the butter in a deep pan, then add the chicken and onion and cook, stirring frequently, for 8 minutes, or until golden brown.

3. Add the rice and mix to coat in the butter. Cook, stirring constantly for 2–3 minutes, or until the grains are translucent. Add the wine and cook, stirring constantly, for 1 minute, until reduced.

4. Mix the saffron with 4 tablespoons of the hot stock. Add the liquid to the rice and cook, stirring constantly, until it has been absorbed.

5. Gradually add the remaining hot stock, a ladleful at a time. Stir constantly and add more liquid as the rice absorbs each addition. Cook for 20 minutes, or until all the liquid has been absorbed and the rice is creamy but still firm to the bite. Season to taste with salt and pepper.

6. Remove the risotto from the heat and add the remaining butter. Mix well, then stir in most the Parmesan cheese until it melts. Spoon the risotto onto warmed plates and serve immediately, sprinkled with the remaining Parmesan cheese.

Venetian Seafood Risotto

SERVES 4

8 oz/225 g mussels, scrubbed and debearded

8 oz/225 g clams, scrubbed

8 oz/225 g large shrimp

2 garlic cloves, halved

1 lemon, sliced

2½ cups water

½ cup butter

1 tbsp olive oil

1 onion, finely chopped

2 tbsp chopped fresh flat-leaf parsley

generous 1½ cups risotto rice

½ cup dry white wine

8 oz/225 g cleaned squid, cut into small pieces or rings

4 tbsp marsala

salt and pepper

1. Discard any mussels and clams with broken shells and any that refuse to close when tapped. Peel the shrimp, reserving the heads and shells. Remove and discard the dark vein. Wrap the heads and shells in cheesecloth and pound with a rolling pin, reserving any liquid they yield.

2. Place the garlic, lemon, mussels, and clams in a pan and add the wrapped shrimp shells and any reserved liquid. Pour in the water, cover, and bring to a boil over high heat. Cook, shaking the pan frequently, for 5 minutes, until the shellfish have opened. Discard any that remain closed. Remove the clams and mussels from their shells and put in a bowl. Strain the cooking liquid into a measuring cup. Top up with water to make 5 cups, then pour this liquid into a pan. Bring to a boil, then reduce the heat and keep simmering gently over low heat while you make the risotto.

3. Melt 2 tablespoons of the butter with the oil in a deep pan. Add the onion and half the parsley and cook over medium heat, stirring occasionally, for 5 minutes, or until softened. Reduce the heat, add the rice, and mix to coat in oil and butter. Cook, stirring constantly, for 2–3 minutes.

4. Add the wine and cook, stirring constantly, for 1 minute, until reduced. Gradually add the hot stock, a ladleful at a time. Stir constantly and add more liquid as the rice absorbs each addition. Cook for 20 minutes, or until all the liquid has been absorbed and the rice is creamy but still firm to the bite.

5. About 5 minutes before the rice is ready, melt 4 tablespoons of the remaining butter in a heavy-bottom pan. Add the squid and cook, stirring frequently, for 3 minutes, then add the reserved shrimp and cook for an additional 2–3 minutes, until the squid is opaque and the shrimp have changed color. Stir in the marsala, bring to a boil, and cook until all the liquid has evaporated. Stir the squid, shrimp, mussels, and clams into the rice, add the remaining butter and parsley, and season to taste with salt and pepper. Heat through briefly and serve immediately.

Second Course

The second course (*secondo piatto*) demonstrates the typical Italian inventiveness with a wide range of meat and fish. As well as the classic steaks and roasts, you'll find interesting braises, such as Osso Bucco with Orange and Lemon. Literally meaning "bone hole," this is made with veal marrowbones sliced in hefty chunks and traditionally topped with a lemon rind and parsley garnish known as *gremolata*. Rosemary-scented pork, roasted until the skin is delectably crisp, is the traditional dish of Umbria. Lamb is often served for special occasions, cooked on a spit or roasted in the oven with wine, garlic, and herbs. Small cutlets from young lambs are a popular delicacy, especially in Rome.

Poultry dishes provide some of Italy's finest food. Every part of the bird is used, including the feet, wings, and innards for making soup.

Chicken alla Cacciatora is a classic braise of chicken, white wine, and tomatoes. Pan-fried chicken breasts are served everywhere, as is spit-roasted chicken strongly flavored with rosemary.

With over 4,350 miles/7,000 km of coastline and numerous inland waterways and lakes, it is hardly surprising that fish and seafood feature highly on the Italian menu. Italians eat everything that comes out of the sea, from the smallest baby fish to the massive tuna. Livorno Seafood Stew typically showcases the wonderful variety of fish and seafood available. In the mountains of the north, river trout are popular, while in the south tuna and swordfish are more likely to be on the menu. Simple techniques, such as broiling or searing, enhance the fresh natural flavors.

Saltimbocca alla Romana

SERVES 4

8 small, thin veal cutlets, about 3 oz/85 g each

8 slices Parma ham

16 sage leaves

all-purpose flour, for coating

4 tbsp butter

¾ cup dry white wine

salt and pepper

1. Place the veal cutlets between 2 sheets of plastic wrap and carefully pound to an even thickness using a meat mallet or rolling pin. Place a slice of Parma ham and 2 sage leaves on top of each cutlet, then fold in half and secure with a wooden toothpick. Spread out the flour on a plate and use to coat the cutlets, tapping off any excess.

2. Melt the butter in a large skillet and cook the cutlets over high heat for 2 minutes on each side. Season to taste with salt and pepper, then sprinkle over 2–3 tablespoons of the wine. Once the wine has evaporated, remove the cutlets from the pan and place on a warmed plate.

3. Pour the remaining wine into the skillet, scraping any sediment from the bottom, and simmer for 1–2 minutes. Pass through a fine-meshed strainer into a pitcher and pour over the cutlets. Serve immediately.

Osso Bucco with Orange and Lemon

SERVES 6

1–2 tbsp all-purpose flour

6 meaty slices osso buco (veal shins)

2 lb 4 oz/1 kg fresh tomatoes, peeled, seeded, and diced, or 1 lb 12 oz/800 g canned chopped tomatoes

1–2 tbsp olive oil

2 onions, finely chopped

2 carrots, finely diced

1 cup dry white wine

1 cup veal stock

6 large basil leaves, torn

1 large garlic clove, finely chopped

finely grated rind of 1 large lemon

finely grated rind of 1 orange

2 tbsp finely chopped fresh flat-leaf parsley

salt and pepper

crusty bread, to serve

1. Place the flour in a plastic bag and season well with salt and pepper. Add the osso bucco, a couple of pieces at a time, and shake until well coated. Remove and shake off the excess flour. Continue until all the pieces are coated. If using canned tomatoes, place in a strainer and let them drain.

2. Heat 1 tablespoon of the oil in a large, ovenproof casserole. Add the osso bucco and cook for 10 minutes on each side, until well browned. Remove from the casserole.

3. Add 1–2 teaspoons of oil to the casserole, if necessary. Add the onions and cook for 5 minutes, stirring, until softened. Stir in the carrots and continue cooking until softened.

4. Add the tomatoes, wine, stock, and basil and return the osso bucco to the casserole. Bring to a boil, then reduce the heat, cover, and simmer for 1 hour. Check that the meat is tender with the tip of a knife. If not, continue cooking for 10 minutes and test again.

5. When the meat is tender, sprinkle with the garlic and the lemon and orange rinds, re-cover, and cook for an additional 10 minutes.

6. Adjust the seasoning, adding salt and pepper if needed. Sprinkle with the parsley and serve with crusty bread.

Veal with Tuna Sauce

1 lb 10 oz/750 g veal loin, boned

2 carrots, thinly sliced

1 onion, thinly sliced

2 celery stalks, thinly sliced

2 cloves

2 bay leaves

4 cups dry white wine

5 oz/140 g canned tuna, drained

4 anchovy fillets, drained and finely chopped

½ cup capers, rinsed and finely chopped

2 oz/55 g gherkins, drained and finely chopped

2 egg yolks

4 tbsp lemon juice

½ cup extra virgin olive oil

salt and pepper

lemon wedges and chopped fresh flat-leaf parsley, to garnish

1. Place the veal in a large, nonmetallic dish and add the carrots, onion, celery, cloves, and bay leaves. Pour in the wine and turn the veal to coat. Cover with plastic wrap and let marinate in the refrigerator overnight.

2. Drain the veal, reserving the marinade, and roll up the meat before wrapping it in a piece of cheesecloth and tying it with string so that it holds its shape. Place the veal in a large pan. Pour the marinade into another pan and bring to a boil. Pour it over the veal and add enough boiling water to cover. Season to taste with salt and pepper, bring back to a boil, then reduce the heat, cover, and let simmer for 1½ hours, until tender but still firm.

3. Transfer the veal to a plate and set aside to cool completely, then let chill until ready to serve. Strain the cooking liquid into a bowl and set aside to cool.

4. Combine the tuna, anchovies, capers, and gherkins in a bowl or process in a food processor or blender to make a paste. Beat the egg yolks with the lemon juice in another bowl. Gradually beat in the oil, adding it drop by drop to start with and then in a steady stream. When all the oil has been incorporated, stir in the tuna mixture and about 2 tablespoons of the cooled cooking liquid to create the consistency of heavy cream. Season to taste with salt and pepper. Cover with plastic wrap and let chill in the refrigerator until required.

5. To serve, unwrap the veal and pat it dry with paper towels. Using a sharp knife, cut the meat into ⅛–½ inch/3–10 mm thick slices and arrange them on a serving platter. Stir the tuna sauce and spoon it over the veal. Garnish with lemon wedges and parsley and serve.

Beef Braised in Red Wine

SERVES 6

3 tbsp olive oil

2 onions, finely sliced

2 garlic cloves, chopped

2 lb 4 oz/1 kg braising beef, cut into thick
  strips

2 tbsp all-purpose flour

1¼ cups good-quality red wine, such as Chianti

2 fresh sage sprigs

scant 1 cup beef or vegetable stock

1 tbsp tomato paste

salt and pepper

1 tbsp finely chopped fresh flat-leaf parsley,
  to garnish

1. Preheat the oven to 300°F/150°C. Heat 1 tablespoon of the oil in a large skillet, then add the onions and garlic and cook over medium heat, stirring frequently, for 6–8 minutes, or until softened and browned. Remove with a slotted spoon and transfer to a casserole.

2. Heat the remaining oil in the skillet, then add the beef and cook over high heat, stirring, for 3–4 minutes, or until browned all over. Sprinkle in the flour and stir well to prevent lumps. Season well with salt and pepper. Reduce the heat to medium, then pour in the wine, stirring constantly, and bring to a boil, continuing to stir constantly.

3. Carefully turn the contents of the skillet into the casserole. Add the sage, stock, and tomato paste, then cover and cook in the center of the preheated oven for 2½–3 hours.

4. Remove from the oven and discard the sage, then taste and adjust the seasoning, adding salt and pepper if needed. Serve immediately, sprinkled with the parsley.

Broiled Steak with Pizzaiola Sauce

SERVES 4

3 tbsp olive oil, plus extra for brushing

1 lb 9 oz/700 g tomatoes, peeled and chopped

1 red bell pepper, seeded and chopped

1 onion, chopped

2 garlic cloves, finely chopped

1 tbsp chopped fresh flat-leaf parsley

1 tsp dried oregano

1 tsp sugar

4 entrecôte or sirloin steaks, about
   6 oz/175 g each

salt and pepper

1. Place the oil, tomatoes, bell pepper, onion, garlic, parsley, oregano, and sugar in a
    heavy-bottom pan and season to taste with salt and pepper. Bring to a boil, reduce the heat,
    and let simmer for 15 minutes.

2. Meanwhile, preheat the broiler. Trim any fat around the outsides of the steaks. Season each
    generously with pepper (but no salt) and brush with oil. Cook under the preheated broiler
    according to taste: 2–3 minutes each side for rare; 3–4 minutes each side for medium; 4–5 minutes
    each side for well done.

3. Transfer the steaks to warmed individual plates and spoon over the sauce. Serve immediately.

Roast Pork Loin

SERVES 6

4 lb/1.8 kg flat piece pork loin, chined (backbone removed) and rind scored

3 garlic cloves, crushed

2 tbsp chopped fresh rosemary, plus 4 sprigs

1 cup dry white wine

salt and pepper

1. Preheat the oven to 450°F/230°C. Put the pork loin on a counter, skin-side down. Make small slits in the meat all over the surface. Season very well with salt and pepper. Rub the garlic all over the meat surface and sprinkle with the chopped rosemary.

2. Roll up the loin and secure the rosemary sprigs on the outside with fine string. Make sure that the joint is securely tied. Season the rind with plenty of salt to create a good crackling.

3. Transfer the meat to a roasting pan and roast in the preheated oven for 20 minutes, or until the fat has started to run. Reduce the oven temperature to 375°F/190°C and pour half the wine over the meat. Roast for an additional 1 hour 40 minutes, basting occasionally with the pan juices.

4. Remove the meat from the oven and let rest in a warm place for 15 minutes before carving. Remove the string and rosemary before cutting into thick slices.

5. Pour off all but 1 tablespoon of the fat from the roasting pan. Add the remaining wine to the pan juices and bring to a boil, scraping up and stirring in any sediment from the bottom of the pan. Spoon over the meat and serve immediately.

Sausages with Cranberry Beans

SERVES 4

2 tbsp virgin olive oil

1 lb 2 oz/500 g luganega or other Italian sausages

5 oz/140 g smoked pancetta or lean bacon, diced

2 red onions, chopped

2 garlic cloves, finely chopped

1⅓ cups dried cranberry beans, covered and soaked overnight in cold water

2 tsp finely chopped fresh rosemary

2 tsp chopped fresh sage

1¼ cups dry white wine

salt and pepper

fresh rosemary sprigs, to garnish

crusty bread, to serve

1. Preheat the oven to 275°F/140°C. Heat the oil in a flameproof casserole. Add the sausages and cook over low heat, turning frequently, for about 10 minutes, until browned all over. Remove from the casserole and set aside.

2. Add the pancetta to the casserole, increase the heat to medium, and cook, stirring frequently, for 5 minutes, or until golden brown. Remove with a slotted spoon and set aside.

3. Add the onions to the casserole and cook over low heat, stirring occasionally, for 5 minutes, until softened. Add the garlic and cook for an additional 2 minutes.

4. Drain the beans and set aside the soaking liquid. Add the beans to the casserole, then return the sausages and pancetta. Gently stir in the herbs and pour in the wine. Measure the reserved soaking liquid and add 1¼ cups to the casserole. Season to taste with salt and pepper. Bring to a boil over low heat and boil for 15 minutes, then transfer to the preheated oven and cook for 2¾ hours.

5. Remove the casserole from the oven and ladle the sausages and beans onto 4 warmed serving plates. Garnish with the rosemary sprigs and serve immediately with crusty bread.

Broiled Leg of Lamb

SERVES 6–8

1 leg of lamb, about 5 lb/2.25 kg, butterflied
4 garlic cloves, crushed
2 tbsp finely chopped fresh rosemary
finely grated rind and juice of 2 lemons

3 tbsp olive oil
salt and pepper
salad greens, to serve

1. Trim any excess fat from the lamb and make small, deep slits in the meat all over the surface. Transfer to a shallow dish and rub all over with the garlic, rosemary, and lemon rind. Pour over the oil and lemon juice and season well with salt and pepper. Cover and let marinate in the refrigerator, or preferably in a pantry or other cool place, for at least 4 hours, or overnight if possible, turning the meat occasionally.

2. Preheat the broiler to high or light a charcoal grill and let burn until the coals are gray and hot. Remove the meat from the marinade and pat dry with paper towels. Season again with salt and pepper and put on the broiler or grill rack. Cook for 2 minutes on each side until sealed, then reduce the heat to medium–high or lift away from the coals and cook for an additional 8 minutes on each side. Test to see if it is cooked to your taste—it should be charred on the outside but still pink in the center.

3. Remove from the heat, then cover with foil and let rest for 15 minutes before carving into long strips. Serve with salad greens.

Chicken alla Cacciatora

SERVES 4–6

1 small chicken, about 3 lb/1.3 kg
2 tbsp olive oil
1 onion, finely chopped
2 oz/55 g pancetta, diced
½ cup dry white wine

4 ripe tomatoes
1 cup chicken stock
salt and pepper
chopped fresh parsley, to garnish

1. Rinse the chicken under cold running water, pat dry with paper towels, and cut into 8 pieces. Rub the skin with plenty of salt and pepper.

2. Heat the oil in a flameproof casserole and cook the onion and pancetta for 3–4 minutes, until the onion is softened and translucent. Add the chicken pieces and fry on all sides, until golden brown. Stir in the wine, bring to a boil, and simmer for 5 minutes.

3. Meanwhile, skin and seed the tomatoes, then dice the flesh. Add to the casserole with the stock, cover, and simmer for 30–40 minutes. Season to taste with salt and pepper and sprinkle with the parsley before serving.

Stuffed Chicken Breasts

SERVES 4

4 skinless, boneless chicken breasts, about
   5½ oz/150 g each

4 thin slices Italian dry-cured ham

4 slices pecorino cheese

4 cooked asparagus spears,
   plus extra to serve

1 tbsp all-purpose flour

3 tbsp butter

2 tbsp olive oil

⅔ cup dry white wine

¼ cup chicken stock

salt and pepper

1. Put each chicken breast between 2 pieces of plastic wrap or inside a plastic food bag and, using a rolling pin, gently beat out until ½ inch/1 cm thick.

2. Season well with salt and pepper and put a slice of ham on top of each chicken breast. Top each with a slice of cheese and an asparagus spear. Roll the breasts up carefully and secure with fine string. Dust with flour and season well with salt and pepper.

3. Heat 2 tablespoons of the butter with the oil in a large skillet. Add the chicken rolls and cook over medium heat, turning frequently, for 15 minutes, or until cooked through, tender, and golden brown. Remove the string, then transfer the chicken rolls to a warmed serving dish and keep warm.

4. Add the wine and stock to the skillet and bring to a boil, scraping up and stirring in any sediment from the bottom of the skillet. Bring to a boil and add the remaining butter. Stir well and let bubble until thick.

5. Spoon the sauce over the chicken and serve immediately with asparagus spears.

Tuna with Salsa Verde

SERVES 4

4 fresh tuna steaks, about
   ¾ inch/2 cm thick
olive oil, for brushing
salt and pepper
lemon wedges, to serve

SALSA VERDE
2 oz/55 g fresh flat-leaf
   parsley, leaves and stems
4 scallions, chopped
2 garlic cloves, chopped
3 anchovy fillets, drained
1 oz/30 g fresh basil leaves
½ tbsp capers, rinsed and dried
2 sprigs fresh oregano or ½ tsp dried oregano
½ cup extra virgin olive oil
1–2 tbsp lemon juice, to taste

1. To make the salsa verde, put the parsley, scallions, garlic, anchovy fillets, basil, capers, and oregano
    in a food processor. Pulse to chop and blend together. With the motor still running, pour in the oil
    through the feed tube. Add lemon juice to taste, then process again. If the sauce is too thick, add a
    little extra oil. Cover and let chill until required.

2. Place a ridged grill pan over high heat until you can feel the heat rising from the surface. Brush the
    tuna steaks with oil and place, oiled-side down, on the hot pan and charbroil for 2 minutes.

3. Lightly brush the top side of the tuna steaks with a little more oil. Use a pair of tongs to turn the
    tuna steaks over, then season to taste with salt and pepper. Continue to cook for an additional
    2 minutes for rare or up to 4 minutes for well done.

4. Transfer the tuna steaks to serving plates, spoon over the salsa verde, and serve with
    lemon wedges.

Trout Fillets with Porcini

SERVES 4

8 wild trout fillets, about 4 oz/115 g each
1 tbsp chopped fresh tarragon
2¼ cups white wine
1 lb 2 oz/500 g fresh porcini mushrooms

½ cup butter
1 small onion, finely chopped
1 tbsp chopped fresh thyme
salt and pepper

1. Rinse the trout fillets, pat dry with paper towels, and rub well with salt and pepper. Place in a bowl with the tarragon and ½ cup of the wine, then cover and let marinate for 30 minutes.

2. Wipe the porcini with damp paper towels and slice into ½ inch/1 cm thick slices. Melt half of the butter in a skillet and cook the onion for 3–4 minutes, until softened and translucent. Add the porcini and cook, stirring, until the juices have evaporated. Stir in the remaining wine with the thyme, season to taste with salt and pepper, and cook over low heat for 10 minutes.

3. Meanwhile, melt the remaining butter in a large, nonstick skillet over medium–high heat. Lift the trout fillets out of the marinade, reserving the marinade, and pat dry with paper towels. Place the trout in the skillet and cook for 3 minutes on each side. Add the reserved marinade to the skillet and bring to a boil.

4. Transfer the trout fillets and any juices to serving plates and spoon over the porcini mixture. Serve immediately.

Sole with Artichokes

SERVES 4

8 small purple artichokes
juice of 1 lemon
½ cup olive oil
4 garlic cloves, thinly sliced
1 cup white wine

1¾ cups fish stock
all-purpose flour, for coating
1 lb 12 oz/800 g sole fillets
1 tbsp finely chopped fresh parsley
salt and pepper

1. Clean the artichokes under cold running water. Trim the stems 1½ inches/4 cm from the bottom, remove the hard outer leaves, and chop off the sharp tips of the remaining leaves. Cut the artichokes lengthwise into strips and immediately place into a bowl of water with the lemon juice. Let stand until ready to cook, then drain and pat dry with paper towels.

2. Heat 6 tablespoons of the oil in a large saucepan and sauté the artichokes for 5 minutes. Add the garlic and cook until golden brown. Pour in the wine and stock, season to taste with salt and pepper, and simmer gently for 20–25 minutes.

3. Spread out the flour on a plate, season to taste with salt and pepper, and use to coat the fish fillets, tapping off any excess. Heat the remaining oil in a large skillet and cook the fish on both sides, until golden and cooked through.

4. Transfer the artichoke mixture to a serving plate and top with the fish. Scatter over the parsley and serve immediately.

Livorno Seafood Stew

SERVES 6

4 red snapper fillets

1 lb/450 g monkfish tail

14 oz/400 g prepared baby squid, rinsed

3 tbsp olive oil

1 onion, finely chopped

2 garlic cloves, finely chopped

2 fennel bulbs, finely sliced

⅔ cup dry white wine

1 lb 5 oz/600 g canned chopped tomatoes

1 lb 2 oz/500 g mussels, scrubbed and debearded

scant 3 cups fish stock

18 large shrimp, peeled and deveined

salt and pepper

2 tbsp finely chopped fresh flat-leaf parsley, to garnish

6 slices ciabatta, toasted, rubbed with garlic, and drizzled with olive oil, to serve

1. Cut the red snapper fillets into thirds. Cut the monkfish into similar-size pieces, cutting the flesh away from the tailbone. Cut the squid into thick rings and set aside the tentacles.

2. Heat the oil in a large pan, then add the onion, garlic, and fennel and cook over medium heat, stirring frequently, for 4–5 minutes, or until starting to soften. Pour in the wine and stir well, then let simmer until almost evaporated. Add the tomatoes and bring to a boil, then reduce the heat and simmer, uncovered, for an additional 10–15 minutes, or until the fennel is tender and the sauce is reduced and thickened.

3. Discard any mussels with broken shells and any that refuse to close when tapped. Bring the stock to a boil in a separate large pan, then add the mussels and cook, covered, over high heat for 3–4 minutes, shaking the pan occasionally, until the mussels have opened. Discard any mussels that remain closed. Strain the mussels, reserving the stock. Remove half the mussels from their shells, discarding the shells. Keep all the mussels warm.

4. Add the reserved stock to the tomato mixture and bring to a boil. Add the snapper, monkfish, squid, and shrimp to the pan and cook for 2–3 minutes, or until the fish are tender and the shrimp have turned pink. Add all the mussels and heat through. Season to taste with salt and pepper.

5. Divide among warmed bowls, sprinkle over the parsley, and serve with the toasted ciabatta.

Stuffed Squid

SERVES 4

4 prepared squid, with tentacles

2 shallots

1 garlic clove

4 oz/115 g cooked ham, finely chopped

3 tbsp cooked rice

1 egg

1 tbsp finely chopped fresh parsley, plus extra
  to garnish

1 tsp grated lemon rind

1 lb 2 oz/500 g fresh tomatoes

1 tbsp olive oil

¾ cup dry white wine

salt and pepper

1. Wash the squid and pat dry with paper towels. Chop the tentacles into small pieces.

2. Finely chop the shallots and garlic, then place in a bowl with the chopped tentacles, ham, rice, egg, parsley, and lemon rind and mix well. Season to taste with salt and pepper. Spoon the mixture into the squid tubes and secure each opening with a wooden toothpick.

3. Skin and seed the tomatoes, then finely dice the flesh. Set aside. Heat the oil in a skillet and cook the stuffed squid on all sides. Add the tomatoes and wine and bring to a boil. Reduce the heat, cover, and simmer for about 45 minutes. Season to taste with salt and pepper. Transfer the squid to serving plates and spoon over the cooking juices. Garnish with parsley and serve immediately.

Vegetables and Salads

In Italy, vegetables and salads are often eaten on their own, either as an antipasti or after the second course, in order to better appreciate their bright fresh flavors, textures, and colors. This is particularly true of salads, but starchy vegetables, such as beans and potatoes, are served with the main course because they complement instead of compete with the flavor of meat and fish.

Vegetables grow in abundance in Italy, and the Italians have put their hearts into using them in the most imaginative and tasty ways. Each region has its specialties—in the south eggplants are a key ingredient in Caponata, a richly flavored sweet-and-sour vegetable medley, while asparagus and chicory are popular in the northeast and are typically served broiled or baked in a gratin. Some vegetables are eaten raw, others are broiled or fried, then usually cooled and

served with a drizzle of olive oil or fresh lemon juice. A surprising number of vegetables are roasted, not just familiar roots but also fennel and green vegetables, such as broccoli spears or romanesco cauliflower—roasting really intensifies their inherently rich, meaty flavors.

The choice of salads is enormous, ranging from a simple dish of mixed salad greens or arugula topped with a few shavings of Parmesan, to Panzanella, the Tuscan bread and tomato salad flavored with basil, vinegar, and olive oil. Also popular are heartier dishes of roasted vegetables or cooked beans dressed with fruity olive oil and herbs. Vegetable salads are always served slightly warm or at room temperature instead of chilled, which dulls the delicious flavors.

Baked Eggplants with Mozzarella and Parmesan

SERVES 4

4 eggplants, trimmed

3 tbsp olive oil, plus extra for oiling

10½ oz/300 g mozzarella cheese, thinly sliced

4 slices prosciutto, shredded (optional)

1 tbsp chopped fresh marjoram

¼ cup grated Parmesan cheese

salt and pepper

TOMATO SAUCE

4 tbsp olive oil

1 large onion, sliced

4 garlic cloves, crushed

14 oz/400 g canned chopped tomatoes

1 lb/450 g fresh tomatoes, peeled and chopped

4 tbsp chopped fresh parsley

2½ cups vegetable stock

1 tbsp sugar

2 tbsp lemon juice

⅔ cup dry white wine

salt and pepper

BÉCHAMEL SAUCE

2 tbsp butter

scant ¼ cup all-purpose flour

1 tsp dry mustard powder

1¼ cups milk

freshly grated nutmeg

salt and pepper

1. Preheat the oven to 375°F/190°C. Oil a large baking dish.

2. To make the tomato sauce, heat the oil in a large skillet. Add the onion and garlic and cook until just beginning to soften. Add the canned and fresh tomatoes, parsley, stock, sugar, and lemon juice. Cover and simmer for 15 minutes. Stir in the wine and season to taste with salt and pepper.

3. Slice the eggplants thinly lengthwise. Bring a large saucepan of water to a boil and cook the eggplant slices for 5 minutes. Drain on paper towels and pat dry.

4. Pour half of the tomato sauce into the prepared baking dish. Cover with half of the cooked eggplants and drizzle with half the oil. Cover with half of the mozzarella, prosciutto, if using, and marjoram. Season to taste with salt and pepper. Repeat the layers.

5. To make the béchamel sauce, heat the butter in a large saucepan. When it has melted, add the flour and mustard powder. Stir until smooth and cook over low heat for 2 minutes. Slowly beat in the milk. Simmer gently for 2 minutes. Remove from the heat and season with a large pinch of nutmeg, and salt and pepper to taste.

6. Pour the sauce over the eggplant mixture, then sprinkle over the Parmesan cheese. Bake in the preheated oven for 35–40 minutes, until golden. Serve.

Caponata

SERVES 4

4 tbsp olive oil
2 celery stalks, sliced
2 red onions, sliced
1 large eggplant, diced
1 garlic clove, finely chopped
5 plum tomatoes, chopped
3 tbsp red wine vinegar

1 tbsp sugar
3 tbsp pitted green olives
2 tbsp capers, drained and rinsed
salt and pepper
4 tbsp chopped fresh flat-leaf parsley,
  to garnish
ciabatta, to serve

1. Heat half the oil in a large, heavy-bottom pan. Add the celery and onions and cook over low heat, stirring occasionally, for 5 minutes, until softened but not colored. Add the remaining oil and the eggplant. Cook, stirring frequently, for about 5 minutes, until the eggplant starts to color.

2. Add the garlic, tomatoes, vinegar, and sugar, and mix well. Cover the mixture with a circle of wax paper and let simmer gently for about 10 minutes.

3. Remove the wax paper, stir in the olives and capers, and season to taste with salt and pepper. Pour the caponata into a serving dish and set aside to cool to room temperature.

4. Just before serving, sprinkle over the parsley to garnish. Serve with ciabatta.

Fennel Gratin

SERVES 4

4 fennel bulbs

1 tbsp lemon juice

2 tbsp butter, plus extra for greasing

2 tbsp all-purpose flour

2 cups lukewarm milk

½ cup heavy cream

2 tbsp white wine

½ tsp freshly grated nutmeg

1½ cups grated fontina cheese

½ cup pine nuts

salt and pepper

1. Preheat the oven to 350°F/180°C. Grease a large baking dish.

2. Trim the fennel, reserving the green leaves. Cut the fennel bulbs into ¼ inch/5 mm thick slices.
    Bring a large saucepan of lightly salted water to a boil. Add the fennel and lemon juice, bring back
    to a boil, and blanch for 3 minutes. Using a slotted spoon, lift out the fennel and transfer to a bowl
    of ice water to stop the cooking. When cool, transfer to a colander and drain well.

3. Melt the butter in a separate pan, add the flour, and cook over low heat, stirring, for 1–2 minutes.
    Gradually add the milk and cream, stirring constantly. Bring to a boil and simmer gently, until
    thickened. Stir in the wine and nutmeg and season to taste with salt and pepper.

4. Place the fennel in the prepared dish, pour over the sauce, and scatter over the fontina cheese.
    Transfer to the preheated oven and cook for 25 minutes, until golden brown.

5. Meanwhile, toast the pine nuts in a dry skillet. Chop the reserved fennel leaves. Scatter the pine
    nuts and fennel leaves over the gratin before serving.

Zucchini Blossom Fritters

⅔ cup self-rising flour
1 tsp baking powder
1 tbsp extra virgin olive oil
1 egg, beaten
generous ¾–1 cup ice water

olive oil, for shallow-frying
16–20 zucchini blossoms
salt and pepper
sea salt flakes and lemon wedges, to serve

1. Sift the flour and baking powder together into a bowl and add the extra virgin olive oil and egg. Stir in enough of the water to make a batter with the consistency of heavy cream (the exact quantity may vary according to the flour used). Season to taste with salt and a little pepper.

2. Pour a shallow layer of olive oil into a large skillet or wok and heat over high heat until hot. Dip the zucchini blossoms briefly in the batter, then add to the oil and cook, in batches, for 2–4 minutes, or until crisp and golden. Remove with a slotted spoon and drain on paper towels. Serve immediately, lightly sprinkled with sea salt flakes and with lemon wedges for squeezing over.

Spinach in Gorgonzola Sauce

SERVES 4

2 lb 4 oz/1 kg spinach
4½ tbsp butter
½ tsp freshly grated nutmeg
½ cup white wine

½ cup milk
generous 1 cup crumbled Gorgonzola cheese
2 egg yolks
salt and pepper

1. Remove and discard any tough stems from the spinach, then place the leaves in a colander and wash under cold running water. Let drain.

2. Melt half the butter in a large saucepan over medium heat. Stir in the spinach, with the water still clinging to its leaves, cover, and cook for 3–4 minutes, until wilted. Stir in the nutmeg and season to taste with salt and pepper, then reduce the heat to low to keep the spinach warm while you prepare the sauce.

3. Pour the wine and milk into a separate pan, bring to a boil, and simmer until reduced slightly. Add the Gorgonzola and stir until melted. Remove from the heat. Beat the egg yolks in a small bowl and stir in a little of the hot sauce, then tip back into the pan with the remaining butter and the spinach. Taste and adjust the seasoning, adding salt and pepper if needed. Serve immediately.

Asparagus Gratin

SERVES 4–6

butter, for greasing
2 lb 4 oz/1 kg asparagus spears
pinch of sugar
115 g/4 oz fontina cheese, sliced

½ cup grated Parmesan cheese
½ cup heavy cream
salt and pepper

1. Preheat the oven to 475°F/240°C. Grease a large baking dish.

2. Wash the asparagus, then cut off and discard the woody ends. Bring a large saucepan of lightly salted water to a boil. Add the asparagus and sugar, bring back to a boil, and simmer for about 15 minutes, until tender but still firm to the bite. Drain.

3. Transfer the asparagus to the prepared baking dish. Place the fontina cheese on top, sprinkle over the Parmesan, and pour over the cream. Bake in the preheated oven for 8 minutes, until the topping is golden brown. Sprinkle with pepper and serve immediately.

Rosemary Potatoes

SERVES 4

3 sprigs fresh rosemary
1 lb 12 oz/800 g small potatoes, cubed
3 garlic cloves, coarsely chopped

5 tbsp olive oil, plus extra for oiling
salt and pepper

1. Preheat the oven to 400°F/200°C. Brush a large baking dish with the oil.

2. Remove the leaves from the rosemary sprigs, discarding the stems, and chop coarsely. Set aside.

3. Place a layer of potatoes in the baking dish, sprinkle over a little of the garlic and rosemary, and season to taste with salt and pepper. Repeat the layers until all the potatoes, garlic, and rosemary have been used up.

4. Drizzle over the oil, then transfer to the preheated oven and cook, stirring occasionally, for 45 minutes, or until the potatoes are tender and lightly browned.

Roasted Vegetable Salad

SERVES 4

1 onion	2–4 tbsp olive oil
1 eggplant	1 tbsp balsamic vinegar
1 red bell pepper, seeded	2 tbsp extra virgin olive oil
1 orange bell pepper, seeded	salt and pepper
1 large zucchini	1 tbsp shredded fresh basil, to garnish
2–4 garlic cloves	Parmesan cheese shavings, to serve

1. Preheat the oven to 400°F/200°C.

2. Cut all the vegetables into even-size wedges, put into a roasting pan, and scatter over the garlic cloves. Pour over 2 tablespoons of the olive oil and toss the vegetables until well coated with the oil. Season to taste with salt and pepper. Transfer to the preheated oven and cook for 40 minutes, or until tender, adding more olive oil if needed.

3. Meanwhile, put the vinegar, extra virgin olive oil, and salt and pepper to taste into a screw-top jar and shake until blended.

4. When the vegetables are cooked, remove from the oven, arrange on a serving dish, and pour over the dressing. Sprinkle with the basil and serve warm or at room temperature with Parmesan cheese shavings.

Panzanella

SERVES 4

8 large ripe tomatoes

2 garlic cloves, crushed

6 tbsp extra virgin olive oil, plus extra to serve

2 tbsp red wine vinegar or balsamic vinegar

8 oz/225 g two-day-old Tuscan saltless bread or other rustic country bread

1 red onion, halved and thinly sliced

small handful of fresh basil leaves, coarsely torn

salt and pepper

1. Halve the tomatoes and remove and discard the seeds, then cut the flesh into eighths. Put in a strainer over a bowl to collect the juice.

2. Add the garlic to the tomato juice and season well with salt and pepper. Pour in the oil and vinegar and stir well.

3. Break the bread up into coarse pieces and put in the bowl, then gently stir until the bread has absorbed all the juice. Rub the bread between your fingers to break it into smaller pieces, handling it carefully to avoid breaking it up too much.

4. Place a layer of the soaked bread in a serving dish and spoon over half the tomatoes and onion. Add another layer of bread and top with the remaining tomatoes, onion, and the basil. Cover and let stand at room temperature for 1 hour for the flavors to be absorbed by the bread.

5. Stir well, then taste and adjust the seasoning, adding salt and pepper if needed. Drizzle with a little extra oil before serving.

Fava Bean and Pecorino Salad

SERVES 6

8 oz/225 g shelled fresh fava beans
5 tbsp extra virgin olive oil
2 tbsp freshly squeezed lemon juice
1 tbsp chopped fresh mint
1½ cups cubed unaged pecorino cheese

3½ cups arugula leaves
½ cup pecorino cheese shavings
salt and pepper

1. If the beans are extremely fresh and tiny, you can serve them raw, but otherwise blanch them for 2–3 minutes in a large pan of boiling water. Drain, then rinse under cold running water and drain again.

2. Put the drained beans in a dish. Pour over the oil and lemon juice, then add the mint. Season well with salt and pepper and mix in the pecorino cheese cubes.

3. Arrange the arugula leaves on a serving dish and spoon over the bean-and-cheese mixture. Sprinkle over the cheese shavings and serve.

Three-Color Salad

SERVES 4

10 oz/280 g mozzarella, drained and thinly
    sliced
8 plum tomatoes, sliced

20 fresh basil leaves
½ cup extra virgin olive oil
salt and pepper

1. Arrange the mozzarella and tomato slices on 4 individual serving plates and season to taste with salt. Set aside in a cool place for 30 minutes.

2. Sprinkle the basil leaves over the salad and drizzle with the olive oil. Season with pepper and serve immediately.

Green and White Bean Salad

½ cup dried great northern beans, soaked
  overnight
8 oz/225 g fine green beans, trimmed
¼ red onion, thinly sliced
12 pitted black olives
1 tbsp fresh snipped chives
salt

DRESSING
½ tbsp lemon juice
½ tsp Dijon mustard
6 tbsp extra virgin olive oil
salt and pepper

1. Drain the soaked beans and put in a saucepan with plenty of fresh water to cover. Bring to a boil, then boil rapidly for 15 minutes. Reduce the heat slightly and cook for an additional 30 minutes, or until tender but not disintegrating. Add salt in the last 5 minutes of cooking. Drain and set aside.

2. Meanwhile, plunge the green beans into a large pan of boiling water. Return to a boil and cook for 4 minutes, until just tender but still brightly colored. Drain and set aside.

3. Mix together the dressing ingredients, then let stand. While both types of beans are still slightly warm, pour them into a shallow serving dish or arrange on individual plates. Scatter over the onion slices, olives, and chives. Stir the dressing and spoon over the salad. Serve immediately, at room temperature.

Beets with Balsamic Vinegar

SERVES 4

1 lb 2 oz/500 g beets
2 tbsp balsamic vinegar
1 tbsp Dijon mustard

5 tbsp olive oil
small bunch of fresh mint
salt and pepper

1. Preheat the oven to 400°F/200°C. Wash the beets and pat dry with paper towels. Wrap each beet individually in aluminum foil, place on a baking sheet, and cook in the preheated oven for 40–60 minutes, depending on size.

2. Remove and discard the foil and let the beets cool slightly. When cool enough to handle, peel the beets—it is advisable to wear a pair of disposable plastic gloves for this job or the juices will stain your hands. Cut the beets into thin slices and transfer to a serving plate.

3. Place the vinegar, mustard, and oil in a small bowl, season to taste with salt and pepper, and mix well. Pour over the beet slices.

4. Finely shred the mint leaves, setting aside a few whole leaves for garnish. Scatter the shredded mint leaves over the beet slices, garnish with the reserved mint leaves, and serve.

Orange Salad

SERVES 4

4 oranges
1 red onion
2 tbsp finely chopped fresh flat-leaf parsley,
  plus extra sprigs to garnish

4 tbsp olive oil
salt and pepper

1. Using a sharp knife, chop the top and bottom off each orange, then remove and discard the peel and white pith. Cut crosswise into thin slices and arrange on a large serving plate.

2. Chop the onion in half through the root, then cut one half of the onion into thin slices. Finely chop the remaining onion half and mix all the onion together with the parsley. Scatter over the orange slices and season with a little salt and pepper. Drizzle over the oil.

3. Cover with plastic wrap and let marinate in the refrigerator for 1 hour. Remove from the refrigerator 5 minutes before serving and garnish with parsley sprigs.

Radicchio Salad

SERVES 4

14 oz/400 g radicchio leaves
1 tbsp olive oil
2 oz/115 g pancetta, cut into small cubes

2 tbsp balsamic vinegar
salt and pepper

1. Wash the radicchio leaves and shake dry. Tear the leaves into bite-size pieces and divide among 4 serving plates.

2. Heat the oil in a skillet over medium heat and cook the pancetta for 4–5 minutes, until crispy. Pour in the vinegar and season to taste with salt and pepper.

3. Drizzle the pancetta mixture over the radicchio and serve immediately.

Bread, Pizza, and Desserts

Good bread is an essential part of the Italian meal—it appears on the table without fail to nibble on while you wait for the first course. Types of breads vary from region to region. Soft spongy *focaccia,* sometimes flavored with onion and rosemary, is immensely popular in Liguria, while *grissini* (dry bread sticks) are a specialty of Piedmont. Italians do not butter their bread; instead they use it to scoop up the sauce remaining in the pasta bowl or tasty meat juices from the main course.

Pizza is known the world over, but to create the irresistible aroma and taste of an authentic Italian pizza you will need homemade dough and freshly-made tomato sauce. A true pizza is crisp and chewy with a soft integral topping that melts into the base. A classic is Pizza Margherita, with its simple topping of tomatoes, mozzarella, and basil, but this

mozzarella, and basil, but this recipe can easily be adapted to use your favorite toppings. Other variations include the Roman-style *pizza bianca,* made without tomatoes, and the stuffed pizza turnover, or *calzone*.

Desserts in Italy are often simple affairs consisting of a bowl of fresh seasonal fruit, or a freshly made fruit salad. However, there are more sumptuous concoctions. Tiramisu and Panna Cotta are well known, but there is also Zuccotto, a dome-shaped molded dessert consisting of liqueur-soaked ladyfingers filled with whipped cream, almonds, and chocolate. The Italians also love cakes and pastries, particularly for special celebrations or to enjoy after a family Sunday lunch.

Focaccia with Onion and Rosemary

MAKES 1 LOAF

1 lb/450 g white bread flour,
  plus extra for dusting

1½ tsp active dry yeast

½ tsp salt

2 tbsp chopped fresh rosemary, plus extra
  sprigs to garnish

5 tbsp extra virgin olive oil, plus extra for oiling

1¼ cups warm water

1 red onion, finely sliced and separated into
  rings

1 tbsp coarse sea salt

1. Mix the flour, yeast, and salt together in a mixing bowl, then stir in the chopped rosemary. Make a well in the center. Mix 3 tablespoons of the oil and the water together in a pitcher and pour into the well. Gradually mix the liquid into the flour mixture with a round-bladed knife. Gather the mixture together with your hands to form a soft dough.

2. Turn the dough out onto a lightly floured counter and knead for 8–10 minutes, or until smooth and elastic. Return the dough to the bowl and cover with a clean dish towel or oiled plastic wrap, then let rise in a warm place for 45 minutes–1 hour, or until doubled in volume. Turn out and gently knead again for 1 minute, or until smooth.

3. Preheat the oven to 400°F/200°C. Oil a cookie sheet. Gently roll the dough out to a circle about 12 inches/30 cm in diameter—it doesn't have to be a perfect circle; a slightly oval shape is traditional. Transfer to the prepared cookie sheet and cover with a clean dish towel or oiled plastic wrap, then let rise in a warm place for 20–30 minutes.

4. Make holes about 2 inches/5 cm apart all over the surface of the dough with the handle of a wooden spoon. Spread the onion rings over the dough, then drizzle with the remaining oil and sprinkle over the sea salt. Bake in the preheated oven for 20 minutes, then scatter over the rosemary sprigs and bake for an additional 5 minutes, or until well risen and golden brown. Transfer to a cooling rack to cool for a few minutes, then serve the bread warm.

Ciabatta

MAKES 3 LOAVES

1¾ cups lukewarm water
4 tbsp lukewarm low-fat milk
4½ cups white bread flour
1 envelope active dry yeast
2 tsp salt
3 tbsp olive oil

BIGA
3 cups white bread flour, plus extra for dusting
1¼ tsp active dry yeast
scant 1 cup lukewarm water

1. First, make the biga. Sift the flour into a bowl, stir in the yeast, and make a well in the center. Pour in the lukewarm water and stir until the dough comes together. Turn out onto a lightly floured counter and knead for 5 minutes, until smooth and elastic. Shape the dough into a ball, put it into a bowl, and put the bowl into a plastic bag or cover with a damp dish towel. Let rise in a warm place for 12 hours, until just beginning to collapse.

2. Gradually mix the water and milk into the biga, beating with a wooden spoon. Gradually mix in the flour and yeast with your hand, adding them a little at a time. Finally, mix in the salt and oil with your hand. The dough will be very wet, but do not add extra flour. Put the bowl into a plastic bag or cover with a damp dish towel and let the dough rise in a warm place for 2 hours, until doubled in volume.

3. Dust 3 cookie sheets with flour. Using a spatula, divide the dough among the prepared cookie sheets without knocking out the air. With lightly floured hands, gently pull and shape each piece of dough into a rectangular loaf, then flatten slightly. Dust the tops of the loaves with flour and let rise in a warm place for 30 minutes.

4. Meanwhile, preheat the oven to 425°F/220°C. Bake the loaves for 25–30 minutes, until the crust is lightly golden and the loaves sound hollow when tapped on the bottom with your knuckles. Transfer to wire racks to cool.

Olive Bread

MAKES 3 SMALL LOAVES

3½ cups white bread flour, plus extra for
    dusting
1 envelope active dried yeast
1 tsp salt
pinch of sugar

1¼ cups lukewarm water
9 oz/250 g Swiss chard, chopped
¾ cup chopped black olives
2 tbsp olive oil, plus extra for brushing

1. Sift the flour into a large bowl and make a well in the center. Pour the yeast, salt, and sugar into the well with the water. Gradually incorporate the flour into the liquid, using your fingers, and bring the mixture together to form a dough. Turn out onto a lightly floured counter and knead the dough for 5–10 minutes, until smooth and elastic. Shape the dough into a ball, put it in the bowl, and cover with plastic wrap. Let rise in a warm place for about 1 hour, until the dough has doubled in volume.

2. Brush a cookie sheet with oil. Punch down the dough with your fist and turn out onto a lightly floured counter. Knead the Swiss chard and olives into the dough and divide into 3 pieces. Form each piece of dough into an oblong loaf and place on the prepared cookie sheet. Dust a clean dish towel with flour, place over the cookie sheet, and let rise for 1 hour.

3. Preheat the oven to 425°F/220°C. Brush the loaves with the oil and bake in the preheated oven for 20–25 minutes. Turn out onto a wire rack and let cool.

Pizza Margherita

MAKES 1 PIZZA

PIZZA DOUGH

1½ cups all-purpose flour, plus extra for
  dusting

1 tsp salt

1 tsp active dry yeast

1 tbsp olive oil, plus extra for brushing and
  drizzling

6 tbsp lukewarm water

TOPPING

¾ cup prepared pizza tomato sauce or
  12 oz/350 g tomatoes, peeled and halved

1 garlic clove, thinly sliced

2 oz/55 g mozzarella cheese, thinly sliced

1 tsp dried oregano

salt and pepper

fresh basil sprigs, to garnish

1. Sift the flour and salt together into a bowl and stir in the yeast. Make a well in the center and pour
   in the oil and lukewarm water. Stir well with a wooden spoon until the dough begins to come
   together, then knead with your hands until it leaves the side of the bowl. Turn out onto a lightly
   floured counter and knead well for 5–10 minutes, until smooth and elastic.

2. Brush a bowl with oil. Shape the dough into a ball, put it into the bowl, and put the bowl into a
   plastic bag or cover with a damp dish towel. Let rise in a warm place for 1 hour, until doubled
   in volume.

3. Brush a cookie sheet with oil. Turn out the dough onto a lightly floured counter, punch down with
   your fist, and knead for 1 minute. Roll or press out the dough to a 10-inch/25-cm circle. Place on the
   prepared cookie sheet and push up the edge slightly all around. Put the cookie sheet in a plastic
   bag or cover with a damp dish towel and let rise in a warm place for 10 minutes.

4. Preheat the oven to 400°F/200°C. Spread the tomato sauce, if using, over the pizza bottom almost
   to the edge. If using fresh tomatoes, squeeze out some of the juice and coarsely chop the flesh.
   Spread them evenly over the pizza bottom and drizzle with oil. Scatter the garlic over the tomato
   layer, then top with the mozzarella cheese. Sprinkle with the oregano and season to taste with salt
   and pepper. Bake in the preheated oven for 15–20 minutes, until the crust is golden brown and
   crisp. Brush the crust with oil, garnish with basil sprigs, and serve immediately.

Calzone

SERVES 4

2 tbsp olive oil, plus extra for brushing
1 red onion, thinly sliced
1 garlic clove, finely chopped
14 oz/400 g canned chopped tomatoes
⅓ cup pitted black olives

2 quantities Pizza Dough (see page 164)
all-purpose flour, for dusting
7 oz/200 g mozzarella cheese, diced
1 tbsp chopped fresh oregano
salt and pepper

1. Preheat the oven to 400°F/200°C. Lightly oil 2 cookie sheets.

2. Heat the oil in a skillet, add the onion and garlic, and cook over low heat, stirring occasionally, for 5 minutes, until softened. Add the tomatoes and cook, stirring occasionally, for an additional 5 minutes. Stir in the olives and season to taste with salt and pepper. Remove the skillet from the heat.

3. Divide the pizza dough into 4 pieces. Roll out each piece on a lightly floured counter to form an 8-inch/20-cm circle.

4. Divide the tomato mixture among the circles, spreading it over half of each almost to the edge. Top with the mozzarella cheese and sprinkle with the oregano. Brush the edge of each circle with a little water and fold over the uncovered sides. Press the edges to seal.

5. Transfer the calzones to the prepared cookie sheets and bake in the preheated oven for about 15 minutes, until golden and crisp. Remove from the oven and let stand for 2 minutes, then transfer to warmed plates and serve.

Grissini

2½ cups white bread flour, plus extra
   for dusting
1½ tsp salt
1½ tsp active dry yeast

scant 1 cup lukewarm water
3 tbsp olive oil, plus extra for brushing
sesame seeds, for coating

1. Lightly oil 2 cookie sheets. Sift the flour and salt together into a warmed bowl. Stir in the yeast and make a well in the center. Add the water and oil to the well and mix to form a soft dough.

2. Turn out the dough onto a lightly floured counter and knead for 5–10 minutes, or until smooth and elastic. Put the dough in an oiled bowl, cover with a damp dish towel, and let rise in a warm place for 1 hour, or until doubled in volume.

3. Turn out the dough again and knead lightly. Roll out to a rectangle measuring 9 x 8 inches/ 23 x 20 cm. Cut the dough into 3 strips, each 8 inches/20 cm long, then cut each strip across into 10 equal pieces.

4. Gently roll and stretch each piece of dough into a stick about 12 inches/30 cm long, then brush with oil. Spread the sesame seeds out on a large, shallow plate or tray. Roll each breadstick in the sesame seeds to coat, then place them, spaced well apart, on the prepared cookie sheets. Brush with oil, cover with a damp dish towel, and let rise in a warm place for 15 minutes. Meanwhile, preheat the oven to 400°F/200°C.

5. Bake the breadsticks in the preheated oven for 10 minutes. Turn over and bake for an additional 5–10 minutes, until golden. Transfer to a wire rack and let cool.

Almond Biscotti

MAKESS 20–30

1⅔ cups whole blanched almonds

scant 1½ cups all-purpose flour, plus extra for dusting

scant 1 cup superfine sugar, plus extra for sprinkling

1 tsp baking powder

½ tsp ground cinnamon

2 eggs

2 tsp vanilla extract

1. Preheat the oven to 350°F/180°C. Line 2 cookie sheets with parchment paper.

2. Coarsely chop the almonds, leaving some whole. Mix the flour, sugar, baking powder, and cinnamon together in a mixing bowl. Stir in all the almonds.

3. Beat the eggs with the vanilla extract in a small bowl, then add to the flour mixture and mix together to form a firm dough.

4. Turn the dough out onto a lightly floured counter and knead lightly. Divide the dough in half and shape each piece into a long, thick log, about 2 inches/5 cm wide. Transfer to the prepared cookie sheets and sprinkle with sugar, then bake in the preheated oven for 20–25 minutes, or until brown and firm.

5. Remove from the oven and let cool for a few minutes, then transfer the logs to a cutting board and cut into ½-inch/1-cm slices. Meanwhile, reduce the oven temperature to 325°F/160°C.

6. Arrange the biscotti slices, cut-sides down, on the cookie sheets. Bake in the oven for 15–20 minutes, or until dry and crisp. Remove from the oven and let cool on a wire rack. Store in an airtight container to keep crisp.

Panforte di Siena

light olive oil, for oiling

¾ cup honey

¾ cup superfine sugar

⅔ cup candied lemon peel,
   finely chopped

⅔ cup candied orange peel,
   finely chopped

generous 1 cup ground almonds

⅔ cup whole blanched almonds, coarsely
   chopped

⅔ cup whole blanched hazelnuts, coarsely
   chopped

generous ⅓ cup all-purpose flour

2 tbsp unsweetened cocoa

1 tsp ground cinnamon

½ tsp ground cloves

a good grating of nutmeg

confectioners' sugar, for dusting

1. Preheat the oven to 325°F/160°C. Oil an 8-inch/20-cm round, shallow cake pan with a removable bottom and line the bottom with parchment paper.

2. Put the honey and sugar in a small pan and heat over low heat, stirring, until the sugar has dissolved.

3. Put the candied citrus peels in a large mixing bowl and add the nuts. Sift in the flour and cocoa and add all the spices. Mix well together. Pour the honey-and-sugar mixture over the dry ingredients and mix well together.

4. Turn the mixture into the prepared pan and press down well so that the surface is smooth. Bake in the preheated oven for 30–40 minutes, or until firm.

5. Remove from the oven and let cool completely in the pan before removing. Dust heavily with confectioners' sugar before serving in slices. The cake will keep in an airtight container or wrapped in plastic wrap and aluminum foil for up to 2–3 months.

Soft Chocolate Cake

SERVES 6–8

10 oz/280 g semisweet chocolate with
  at least 72% cocoa solids, broken into pieces
10 tbsp unsalted butter, plus extra for greasing
4 eggs, separated

¼ cup superfine sugar
generous 2 tbsp all-purpose flour
1 tsp vanilla extract
unsweetened cocoa, for dusting

1. Preheat the oven to 350°F/180°C. Grease an 8-inch/20-cm round, springform cake pan and line the bottom with parchment paper.

2. Put the chocolate and butter in a heatproof bowl, then set the bowl over a pan of barely simmering water and heat until melted. Remove the bowl from the heat and let cool for 5 minutes.

3. Beat the eggs yolks and sugar together in a mixing bowl with a handheld electric mixer until thick and creamy. In a separate mixing bowl, beat the egg whites until thick and glossy.

4. Fold the egg yolk mixture into the melted chocolate. Sift in the flour and fold in together with the vanilla extract. Gently fold in the beaten egg whites.

5. Turn the mixture into the prepared pan and bake in the preheated oven for 15–20 minutes. Do not overcook—the top should be firm but the center still slightly gooey. Remove from the oven, cover, and let cool overnight.

6. Remove the cake pan and peel away the lining paper from the bottom. Dust the surface of the cake with cocoa and serve in slices.

Zuccotto

2 store-bought sponge flan shells

3 tbsp lemon liqueur

2½ cups heavy cream

scant 1 cup confectioners' sugar, plus extra
  for dusting

100 g/3½ oz semisweet chocolate, finely
  grated

1 cup chopped almonds

1. Using a serrated knife, cut the rims off the flan shells to make them an even thickness. Cut 1 flan shell into 12 wedges and use to line a large bowl. Sprinkle over 2 tablespoons of the liqueur.

2. In a large bowl, whip together the cream and confectioners' sugar until stiff. Transfer half the cream mixture to a separate bowl and stir in the chocolate, then spoon into the lined bowl and smooth the surface. Stir the almonds into the remaining cream mixture and spoon on top of the chocolate layer, smoothing the surface. Place the second flan shell on top, press down lightly, and sprinkle over the remaining liqueur. Transfer to the freezer for at least 6 hours.

3. To serve, turn out onto a serving plate and dust with confectioners' sugar.

Sicilian Cassata

SERVES 12

2½ cups ricotta cheese

2 tbsp orange flower water

1½ cups granulated sugar

1 cup water

10½ oz/300 g candied fruit, finely chopped

3½ oz/100 g semisweet chocolate, finely chopped

½ cup chopped pistachio nuts

2 store-bought sponge flan shells

4 tbsp cherry liqueur

2 tbsp lemon juice

1. Mix together the ricotta and orange flower water until smooth. Place 1 cup of the sugar and the water in a small saucepan and place over medium heat until the sugar has dissolved. Simmer until reduced slightly, making sure that it does not burn. Remove from the heat and let cool slightly. Stir into the ricotta mixture with half the candied fruit, the chocolate, and pistachio nuts.

2. Using a serrated knife, cut the rims off the flan shells to make them an even thickness. Cut 1 flan shell into 12 wedges and use to line a large bowl. Sprinkle over 2 tablespoons of the liqueur. Spoon the ricotta mixture into the lined bowl and smooth the surface. Place the second flan shell on top and press down lightly. Transfer to the refrigerator and let chill for at least 5 hours, until firm. Turn out onto a serving plate.

3. Place the remaining sugar in a saucepan with the remaining liqueur, the lemon juice, and a little water. Heat gently until the sugar has dissolved and the liquid is reduced and syrupy. Pour the syrup over the cassata, then decorate with the remaining candied fruit. Chill in the refrigerator for an additional hour before serving.

Quick Tiramisu

SERVES 4

1 cup mascarpone cheese or soft cheese

1 egg, separated

2 tbsp plain yogurt

2 tbsp superfine sugar

2 tbsp dark rum

2 tbsp cold strong black coffee

8 ladyfingers

2 tbsp grated semisweet chocolate

1. Put the mascarpone cheese, egg yolk, and yogurt in a large bowl and beat together until smooth.

2. Whip the egg white in a separate, grease-free bowl until stiff but not dry, then beat in the sugar and gently fold into the cheese mixture. Divide half the mixture among 4 sundae glasses.

3. Mix the rum and coffee together in a shallow dish. Dip the ladyfingers into the rum mixture, break them in half, or into smaller pieces if necessary, and divide among the glasses.

4. Stir any remaining coffee mixture into the remaining cheese mixture and divide among the glasses.

5. Sprinkle with the grated chocolate. Serve immediately or cover and chill in the refrigerator until required.

Stuffed Peaches with Amaretto

SERVES 4

4 tbsp butter

4 peaches

2 tbsp light brown sugar

2 oz/55 g amaretti cookies or macaroons, crushed

2 tbsp amaretto

light cream, to serve

1. Preheat the oven to 350°F/180°C. Use 1 tablespoon of the butter to grease an 8-inch/20-cm gratin dish, or a baking dish large enough to hold 8 peach halves in a single layer.

2. Halve the peaches and remove and discard the pits. If you like, you can skin the peaches by adding them to a heatproof bowl of boiling water for 10–15 seconds, then transferring them with a slotted spoon to a bowl of cold water. When cool enough to handle, peel away the skins.

3. Beat the remaining butter and the sugar together in a bowl until creamy, then add the cookie crumbs and mix well.

4. Arrange the peach halves, cut-side up, in the prepared baking dish, and fill the pit cavities with the cookie mixture. Bake in the center of the preheated oven for 20–25 minutes, or until the peaches are tender.

5. Pour over the amaretto and serve hot with the cream.

Zabaglione

SERVES 4

5 egg yolks
½ cup superfine sugar

⅔ cup marsala or sweet sherry
crushed amaretti cookies, to serve (optional)

1. Place the egg yolks in a large mixing bowl. Add the sugar and beat until the mixture is thick and pale and has doubled in volume.

2. Place the bowl containing the egg yolk-and-sugar mixture over a saucepan of gently simmering water.

3. Add the marsala and beat until the mixture has warmed through and is light and frothy. This process may take as long as 10 minutes.

4. Pour the mixture into heatproof serving glasses and sprinkle over the crushed amaretti cookies, if using. Serve warm.

Panna Cotta

SERVES 6

1 tbsp vegetable oil
1 vanilla bean
2½ cups heavy cream
4 tbsp superfine sugar

2 tsp powdered gelatin
3 tbsp cold water
12 strawberry halves, to decorate

1. Brush 6 x ½-cup baking dishes or ramekins with the oil.

2. Split the vanilla bean with a sharp knife and scrape out all the seeds. Put the bean and the seeds in a pan with the cream and sugar and stir well over low heat. Carefully bring to simmering point and simmer gently for 2–3 minutes. Remove from the heat and let cool a little.

3. Soak the gelatin in the cold water in a small, heatproof bowl. Place the bowl over a pan of gently simmering water and stir until the gelatin has dissolved and the liquid is clear.

4. Remove the vanilla bean from the cream and stir in the gelatin mixture. Pour into the prepared dishes, cover with plastic wrap, and let chill for at least 3 hours, or overnight, until set.

5. To serve, dip the dishes up to the rim (do not immerse completely) in hot water for 2 seconds and then turn out onto serving plates. Serve decorated with the strawberry halves.

Citrus Granita

SERVES 6

6 oranges
1½ lemons
¾ cup granulated sugar

2 cups water
amaretti cookies, to serve

1. Pare the rind from the fruit, then cut off and discard the pith. Slice a few thin strips of rind and set aside separately from the large pieces. Squeeze the juice from the fruit.

2. Boil the sugar and water in a heavy-bottom pan and stir until the sugar has dissolved. Boil, without stirring, for 10 minutes, until syrupy. Remove from the heat, stir in the large rind pieces, cover, and let cool.

3. Strain the cooled syrup into a freezerproof container and stir in the juice. Freeze, uncovered, for 4 hours, until slushy.

4. Blanch the thin strips of rind in a pan of boiling water for 2 minutes. Drain and refresh with cold water. Pat dry with paper towels.

5. Remove the granita from the freezer and break up with a fork. Return to the freezer for an additional 4 hours, until solid.

6. Remove the granita from the freezer and let stand at room temperature until slightly softened. Beat with a fork, then spoon into glasses and decorate with the strips of rind. Serve with amaretti cookies.

Index